MERTHYR HISTORIAN
Volume Eighteen

Merthyr Tydfil Historical Society
South Wales
2005

Registered Charity No 509392
ISBN 0-9544201-4-4

T.F. Holley Ph.D
Chairman and Editor
Merthyr Tydfil Historical Society
52 Chester Close
Heolgerrig
Merthyr Tydfil
CF48 1SW

J. D. Holley
Assistant Editor and Volunteer Typesetter

CONTENTS

Page

IF IT HADN'T BEEN FOR MR HARRIS...........
THE STORY OF A PIT AND ITS TOWN.
by
RAYMOND JONES

Yes, if it hadn't been for Mr Harris.....or for Mr and Mrs Thomas, Mr Nixon, Mr Hill, Mr Kirkhouse and the combined dynasties of Guests and Crawshays and many others, the establishment of villages and towns in the Merthyr Valley and their industrial, social and cultural history might have been very different.

Would there have been a pit or community established among the farmlands of Graigberthlwyd towards the end of the 19th century? It is inconceivable that some entrepreneur would not have seen the potential wealth beneath the surface and sought to exploit it.

However, this is unnecessary conjecture; the entrepreneurs did arrive and it was Mr Harris who, in the early 1870's, made his decision to sink a very deep Pit in the area, which was soon to bear his name—Tre Harris, Town of Harris.

In the course of the following one hundred years a vibrant community became established with its focus on Harris's Colliery. What follows is the story of the Pit and the people who depended on it.

A few scattered farms existed in the immediate area prior to Mr Harris's arrival. In the numeration of Parish Registers, 1811, only a hamlet existed in this area with 27 families made up of 62 males and 66 females. All were employed in agriculture. Later, in the 1870's, there were settlements in the Graigberthlwyd area and in Old Quakers' Yard, nearby. These inhabitants witnessed the coming of Mr F.W. Harris and his associates and were to be astonished by the speed and tenacity of the undertaking, which was to completely transform the neighbourhood and establish " a town of no inconsiderable proportions." (1)

After the purchase of the land from Twyn-y-Garreg Farm, Messrs Harris's Navigation Company set about recruiting sinkers for the task of creating two shafts, north and south.

To accommodate these workmen 32 wooden Huts were built. These were, in the main, one storey dwellings with a large living room and one or two bedrooms and a rent of approximately 6d per week. The occupants relied on a small spring for their water. Astonishingly, these Huts were variously occupied by a succession of inhabitants for more than a further eighty years. As the years went by Hut number 1 had part of the accommodation adapted as a bakery; Hut number 14 served as a day school with religious services taking place on Sundays.

By the 1950's only 28 of the original Huts remained. When one of the dwellings became vacant it was not re-let. The Merthyr Council offered alternative accommodation to the remaining residents, but there was a great resistance to moving from the Huts. By 1960 only one Hut remained and the aged tenant was extremely reluctant to move.

One re-located resident, Mrs Elizabeth Brimble, had lived in the Huts at number 1. Ten of her children were born there. To accommodate this large family the bakery had been converted to make a third bedroom which meant that an extra 3/- a month was added to the rent. A local resident recalled that Mrs Brimble would stand at the door counting her children as they entered the Hut. The children were kept spotlessly clean-"as white as the driven snow." (2)

Other residents had more stories to tell of life in the Huts. Mrs Elizabeth Jane Glass, a 72 year-old widow who lived at number 27, was herself born there and raised six children. Her father, Mr Thomas Williams, known as "Tom Llanidloes" was one of the original tenants of the Huts. Her sister, Mrs Sarah Ellen Hollister, aged 75, was also born there and lived at number 25. When asked to move, Mrs Glass replied, "No, I have lived here all my life and my sister and I want to end our days here."

Today, there is very little evidence that the Huts - the very first dwellings of the embryonic Treharris - ever existed and a very valuable part of the town's heritage has been lost. But a few photographs exist to remind us of how things started in the Pit town.

The Huts

Young and old. The boy standing in front of one of the last of the Huts is Peter Williams of Nelson. He became a Loughborough University graduate and Mechanical Engineer.

Following the erection of the Huts a handsome mansion and numerous cottages were built. Shops began to appear to serve the needs of the expanding population and, predictably, a "most spacious and splendid hotel" (3) was soon completed at an estimated cost of £4,000. The ground floor had a conspicuous ornamental porch and the "admirable bar was fifty feet long, divided into four compartments, with one continuous counter." (4).

Not all local residents were happy with the growth of hotels and public houses which were seen as dens of iniquity. Mrs Mary Jenkins of nearby Pentwyn had this to say in 1881 "...speaking of ungodliness, this is a place for all sorts of sin, the lowest members of society have gathered here, and we have never heard such profanity in this neighbourhood." (5)

A further homily followed from Mary, on recalling the events surrounding the death of a local resident (R.E.). He was found half-dead on the roadside and having been carried to the Angel Inn, he died within a few minutes. "It had been cold and stormy the night before, and he, being drunk, had fallen down and nearly froze to death on the spot. Here again is a lesson for all drunkards."(6)

For good or ill the growing community had to accommodate a range of social amenities in the ensuing years. The continuing expansion of the town depended on one single factor...the success of Mr Harris's mining venture. The sinking of the two shafts to a considerable depth met with a problem, which was to remain a challenge throughout the Pit's existence… water. It was reported in 1879 that something in the order of 1,400 gallons of water were entering the pit every minute. The workings were 200 yards deeper than in any other Colliery in the South Wales coalfield. The South pit descended to 769 yards whilst the North pit seams were 6 or 8 yards nearer the surface. These great depths and the inflow of considerable volumes of water called for urgent action. The first strategy was to order a Cornish pumping engine from the Perran Foundry, Truro. This lifted 230 gallons of water per stroke. The water was removed in a series of "lifts" located at different depths from the surface i.e. at 107, 196, 288, 381 and 467 yards.

Much later in the Pit's history one pump was located part-way down the shaft in a specially created area known as the "Castle." (Mr D.G.C. Phillips, a Treharris resident, in a memoir held at the South Wales Miners' Library states that the "Castle" is more correctly named "Castell" after the man who cut out the cavern from solid rock). The main cavern was 70 yards long, 30 yards wide and 5 yards high.

The water from the bottom of the pit was pumped to, and temporarily stored in, the Castle before being pumped to the surface.

On a personal note my father-in-law, Mr Glyn Williams of Cilhaul, was one of the pumpsmen who, daily, tended the pumps at the Castle. The cage which descended the shaft at the start of his shift carried him as the sole occupant. The cage stopped at the entrance to the Castle long enough for Mr Williams to jump across to his place of work. At the end of the shift the process was reversed. Mr Williams retired from this very responsible position in 1968.

Throughout the working life of the Pit the water was pumped to the surface where it was stored in a reservoir known locally as the Pit Pond. On September 25th, 1886 a remarkable act of bravery took place in the Pit Pond. A seven year old boy fell into the Pond while blackberrying. An onlooker, eleven year old Tommy Rees, plunged into the 11 feet deep pond, swam 100 yards and rescued the younger boy from drowning.

The Royal Humane Society awarded a Bronze Medal to Tommy Rees.

The scholars at the Board School took a deep interest in this act of bravery and several of them wrote a composition exercise on the subject. The Schoolmaster, Mr Henry Davies, released the following exercise written by Tommy Rees to the local newspaper. It makes interesting and moving reading:

"During the times of the blackberries, a little boy seven years of age fell into a reservoir by reaching for some. Thomas Israel screamed out that David Walter Davies was drowning. At once we ran to his assistance, and I told Lewis Samuel to cut my bootlaces and garters while I was pulling off my coat. When he had done that I plunged into the water and caught hold of his scarf and brought him to the side of the pond. The boys who were on the bank caught hold of the little boy's hand and got him up to the grass. Then we carried him home. On the way we put him down to try if he could walk. He was not able to stand on his feet. Then we carried him again till we came to his house. His mother then undressed him, put him in warm water and mustard, and carried him to bed. I was very glad that we were able to save him from drowning, and he was very glad, too, although he asked once –will I die?

4

I was not willing to go to Merthyr to have my photo taken, for fear I should lose the watch offered for regular attendance at school. I have one watch for myself, and wanted another for my brother."(7)

It is no surprise that this young man should grow up to become a pillar of the community. In adulthood he was one of the best known ambulance men in South Wales. He was a serving brother of the Order of St John, Secretary of the Taff Valley Corps, and a Superintendent of the Treharris Division. He was also a trustee of the Ambulance Hall and was largely responsible for the successes gained by the Treharris Ambulance & Cadet teams at the Welsh National Eisteddfodau and other competitions. For over 30 years he was employed as a checkweigher at the Ocean Colliery, Treharris. He was an officer of the local South Wales Miners' Federation Lodge.

To return to the history of the Pit:

By 1881, after overcoming problems of water and of penetrating the hard Pennant strata, the South pit was raising coal in production quantities. .

Treharris in 1891. A print taken from a painting once possessed by John Aurelius, The Navigation Hotel, Treharris

Production tonnage of coal in 1886 measured 343,088 tons. In 1892 the amount was 281,484 tons with a further 301,590 tons raised in 1893.

However, declining coal production left the Harris Company in debt.

Negotiations with the Ocean Coal Company which had started in 1890 were re-opened in 1893. "Experienced Managers" Jacob Ray and John Owen visited Treharris on a tour of inspection. They found that "the coal is good"...and the roadways are "in fair condition," also "the gradients..are very fair" and "horses were working 2 drams a journey."

The consequence of this report was that the Ocean Company was advised to take over Mr Harris's Pit and this it did on 17 January 1893.

Terms of resumption (of work) were drawn up and by July of that year rules and regulations governing working practices were compiled. The final paragraph of the document stated "...each workman will attend his work regularly, and perform it in an efficient, faithful and workmanlike manner, before he is entitled to payment."

A key negotiator in the "take over" was Mr William Jenkins, an official of the Ocean Coal Company. In his report to the Directors of 7 July, 1893, he had some stern words: " A serious amount of hard work has to be done to bring the Colliery to sustain itself, not the least being the institution of a better discipline among the workmen, generally, in place of the evidently existing lax discipline."

Mr Jenkins also estimated that from £8,000 to £10,000 would be needed to make the bottom of the shafts satisfactory.

The newly named "Deep Navigation" Colliery was soon in full production. In the three years from 1895 the annual tonnage of coal raised was 436,813, 452,241 and 596,000, with 2,500 men employed.

Stonebreakers were included in the workforce. Their task was to provide durable surface materials for the roadways in the underground workings. Their pay was one shilling a day!

The stonebreakers and the colliers were often referred to by "nicknames" which sometimes referred to their original home area e.g. Dai Jones Cardi, Hugh the Northman, Tom Jones Ogmore, Jack Hereford, Jim Gloucester etc. Often more picturesque appellations were applied.... Shoni Bully, Jimmy the Rogue, Morriston Monkey, William Jones Groano and Willy Black Pipe.

By 1902 The Ocean Coal Company had invested a further £600,000 in the Deep Navigation Colliery. Labour-saving and highly modernised equipment was introduced into the mine with the purpose of producing coal quickly and economically. Output in that year was 327,000 gross tons with a workforce of 2,000 men each receiving, on average, wages of 28 shillings a week. The work was greatly aided by the presence of over 100 ponies, many working underground but with some doing duty on the surface.

The horses were of varying sizes to suit the type of work required of them with their schedules overseen by the ostlers. Each ostler had the care of his horses as a top priority. Grooming, feeding and stabling were carefully controlled by the ostler who also influenced the speed with which the drams were delivered to the miners. It was very much in the miners' interest to keep on good terms with the ostler since wages depended on filling regularly-delivered empty drams with coal.

In the early years the horses remained permanently below the surface and never saw the light of day. Much later the pit ponies were brought to the surface, once a year, during the "Miners' Fortnight" when the workers left the Pit for their annual holiday.

Pit ponies underground

The following advertisement for the Ocean Coal Company appeared in 1913:
"This coal is unrivalled for Steam Navigation and Railway purposes. It is well known in all the Markets of the world for Economy in consumption, Its Purity and Durability. Ocean (Merthyr) Steam Coal, solely, was used by the Cunard Company Steamers Mauretania and Lusitania in creating a Record for the most Rapid Atlantic Passages.
The Ocean Company supply the requirements of the English Admiralty for trial trips, for the use of the Royal yachts and other special purposes." (8).The advertisement goes on to highlight a particular innovation at Deep Navigation - the construction of the Pit-head Baths. Prior to 1916 miners, at the end of each shift, returned home in their working clothes, often bathing in a tub or tin bath in front of the kitchen fire. The women of the household, wives or sisters, had the never- ending task of washing the coal-dust laden clothes and also of preparing the baths and emptying them after use.

Miner bathing at home. Source unknown.

In 1916 the first Pit-head Baths in the South Wales Coalfield were installed at Deep Navigation, Treharris. This had the most profound effect on the social conditions prevailing in the town. It is not hard to imagine the great relief in each household when the men returned home at the end of the shift showered and in clean clothes.

Interior of the new Pit-head Baths 1916.

In 1932 more modern Baths were installed at the Colliery, the old Baths becoming the Lamp Room. This situation remained during the rest of the life of the Pit.

Before this time cultural and religious life, too, was becoming manifest in the fast-growing community. The growth of Chapels and Churches began quite soon after the Colliery was in full production. In 1881 Brynhyfryd was built to cater for the spiritual needs of the Welsh Baptists in the locality. The foundation stone is still visible having been laid by C.H. James Esq M.P. in May 15, 1882.

The English Baptist cause was established following a meeting in the Huts in 1877. Later the worshippers met in a Trelewis house. Thereafter a permanent building was completed in John Street in 1880.

Tabernacle Chapel was opened in 1893; seven memorial stones in the outer walls of the building commemorate the event.

Memorial stone, Brynhyfryd Chapel 1882

Seion Chapel was built in 1893 and the Wesleyan Methodist Church was completed in 1900. St Mathias Church was erected in 1896 at a cost of £3,500.

It is evident that religious observances were well established very early-on in the history of Treharris. Cultural activities, many originating in the Chapels and Churches, were also soon in evidence. Local resident Mary Jenkins wrote that on Monday 1st August, 1881, " The Great Eisteddfod of Treharris has created quite a stir in the neighbourhood. There has been a United Choir with 200 voices formed between Treharris, Craigberthlwyd and Quakers' Yard, under the conductorship of Eos Cynon who is working in the pits. The musical judge is Carodog and the main piece is the Hallelujah Chorus. Prize is £20.0.0 and a gold medal worth £5.0.0 for the Conductor." (9)

Five choirs competed, with Mountain Ash Choir winning the first prize. Three Brass Bands took part and it was the Cymmer Brass Band which won the event playing a medley of Welsh Folk Tunes.

The local author-celebrity Craigfryn is reported to have won half the prize of £2 for a descriptive song about Treharris.

(Isaac Craigfryn Hughes, a native of Graigberthlwyd who was largely self-taught, gained literary distinction as an author - particularly for the story of *Y Ferch o Gefn Ydfa* - The Maid of Cefn Ydfa. Craigfryn became the secretary of the Treharris Workmen's Library and Secretary of the Graig Lodge of the Miners' Federation).

Interestingly, Mary Jenkins recorded the fact that "Mr Harris, the Squire of the village is giving £25.0.0 for the object of....the Grand Eisteddfod of Treharris." Presumably, Squire Harris was *the* Mr Harris who was the founding father of the township.

10

The continued rapid growth of Treharris is faithfully documented in the various Kelly Directories for South Wales. In the 1901 edition, Schools, a Police Station, a Cemetery and a Public Hall and Institute are highlighted.

- "Board School erected in 1882 and enlarged in 1896. Mr Benjamin P. Evans (Master), Miss Mary Simmons (Mistress) and Miss Lydia Griffiths (Infants' Mistress) were responsible for the education of 480 boys, 360 girls and 500 infants."
- "The South Wales and Monmouthshire Truant School was built near the Quakers' Yard Railway Station in 1893 to accommodate 90 boys ."

(The school was still fully functional in the 1950's before eventually becoming transformed into a Residential Home for Senior Citizens.)

- "The Police Station, in Edward Street, erected in 1886, affords quarters for a sergeant and four constables."
- "the Cemetery of five acres....was opened in 1888, and is near Quakers' Yard station. It is named Beechgrove Cemetery and has a caretaker named Thomas Thomas."
- "The Public Hall and Institute, in the centre of the village, was built in 1892 at a cost of £3,300. The building includes a reading room, library, recreation and committee rooms. The library and reading rooms are supported by contributions from the workmen's wages. The library contains about 1400 volumes, and the reading rooms are supplied with several daily and weekly papers."

Kelly's Directory entry contains this summary in 1901 :
Treharris is "expanding rapidly into a town and consists of well-built workmen's cottages, numerous places of business and well-lit streets. The place is lighted with gas."
There were, indeed, "numerous places of business" - something in excess of 80 establishments. There were 17 grocers, 9 drapers, 9 shopkeepers, 8 bootdealers, 6 butchers, 4 hair dressers, 4 watch makers and 3 ironmongers. Additionally there were builders, carpenters, saddlers and an undertaker. Interestingly 7 farmers are listed. The traders include a good sprinkling of Welsh names-10 Thomases, 7 Joneses and 7 Davieses. The Jewish community seems to have been represented by Samuel Fagot (watchmaker), Solomon Grwsener (furniture dealer) and Samuel Joseph (pawnbroker). At this stage there was no Italian presence in the town, but this was remedied in later years by the presence of "Brachi's" owned in the 40's onwards by the Conti, Opel and Spinetti families.
The continued growth of Treharris depended, fundamentally, on the success of the Deep Navigation Colliery. From its earliest beginnings it was controlled not by the workforce but by the Owners.
Working conditions were never less than hazardous and this fact was very well known to every member of the community. One mother of a miner was to write, "These pits are terrible places, there are many accidents happening here and not much attention

given to any man who is injured. Only barely enough to carry the victim home is allowed out of the pit."(10).

Miners were soon to attempt to improve their working conditions and their pay by joining together to form a Union.

On 2nd August, 1893 hauliers at the Ocean Coal Company pits came out on strike over wages. They were joined by most of the South Wales miners. Police and soldiers kept order for the Owners and by 7th September the strike ended.

In 1897 miners tried to end the "sliding scale" method of payment. In this system miners' pay was fixed according to the selling price of coal.

The Owners locked them out, again calling in the police and troops for protection. After much hardship the miners returned to work.

In 1898 the South Wales Miners' Federation was formed. Two years later Keir Hardie was returned as the first working class Independent Labour M.P. for Merthyr Tydfil - the ward which included Treharris.

By 1905 the Federation had negotiated an agreement with the Owners over wage rates and disputes. Deep Navigation Colliery was party to this Agreement.

In the ensuing five years the Federation fought to improve working conditions for miners in the South Wales Coalfields. Yet, by the autumn of 1910, most Welsh Pits were on strike. The Tonypandy Riots were to follow.

For the next two years the Federation tried to secure agreement over a minimum wage for miners but with no success. The great Strike of 1912 followed and there may well have been unrest in Treharris as the photograph of two policemen at Ocean Deep Navigation Pit suggests.

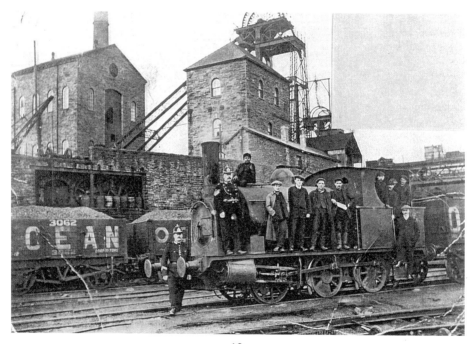

"The Coal Mines (Minimum Wage) Act, 1912 And After" enabled the miners to return to work at wages fixed for each class of underground workmen. The daily wage for a collier in charge of a working place was 4 shillings and 7pence, an ostler received 3 shillings and 2 pence and underground pumpsmen 3 shillings and 4 pence.

The workforce in 1910.

Industrial relations in the coalfield, however, remained volatile and following yet another lock-out in 1921, the exasperated officials of the South Wales Miners' Federation took a very bold step. Whilst the action taken doesn't relate directly to Treharris Pit, nevertheless the Treharris miners were members of the Federation and, presumably, were aware of the action taken by their representatives. The story seems worth relating.

The action took the form of a letter written by Thomas Bell of the Federation to none other than Lenin informing him that the Federation had voted by 120 to 63 to affiliate with the Third International.

This prompted a reply from Lenin in which he expressed the hope that this " is the beginning of a real proletarian mass movement in Great Britain in the communist sense." Lenin further warned that "English capitalists are shrewd, clever, astute" and whilst apologising for his bad English, exhorted the Federation to "start a daily paper of the working class, for the working class." (11).

The workforce at Deep Navigation never identified very strongly with Communism, but were always staunchly Labour supporters. The banner of the Treharris Lodge of the

National Union of Miners carried the embroidered message "Towards a Socialist Britain and World Peace."

Interestingly, in the early years of the 21st Century, when no trace of Treharris Pit remains, this banner proudly leads the procession from the town to the Millennium Park at the start of the annual Treharris Festival.

Many banners from the pit villages and towns ended up in the South Wales Miners' Library, but Treharris retained its banner. It also retained the Pit hooter, which is now housed in a garage near Brynhyfryd Chapel. It is sounded on high days and holidays!

The General Strike of 1926 had a profound effect on the inhabitants of all the Valley towns and villages. Although officially called off after nine days, the miners, who were not consulted, remained out of work for a further seven months. On May 4th buses and the trains stopped running, the miners left work and pit ponies were brought to the surface.

Treharris had one of the four district strike committees in the Borough. It was composed of miners, railwaymen and other workers. Help was received from colliery officials. Sub-committees were formed for food, finance, permits and sport and recreation. Relief notes for 6 shillings were issued to financial members of the South Wales Miners' Federation.

Treharris Silver Band, which in 1922 had become the Champion Record Holder of Wales with 22 First Prizes, played concerts in aid of the district relief fund and collected £310 by early July.

Treharris Silver Band 1922

Other fund-raising events were held in the months of gloriously sunny weather. Huw Williams in his article in *Merthyr Historian*, Volume 2, describes the strike as " a story of jazz bands, summer sports, concerts and soup kitchens." Perhaps the highlight of all the activity was the splendid carnival procession held in Cyfarthfa Park in early August.

Jazz band fever had, by this time, infected all the towns and villages in the Borough. The Coons Jazz Band of Aberfan (Bryntaf) were to become British & Colonial Champions in 1934. Not to be outdone Treharris formed a Zulu Warriors Band, which marched in the Cyfarthfa Carnival, together with the Japs and Pengarn Negro Bandsmen and many more in the mile-long procession. At the end of September fifty jazz bands took part in a festival at Quakers' Yard in aid of local distress funds.

Treharris Zulus

Although known locally as the "jazz band strike" it was not all fun and frolic in the valleys during those summer months. Extreme hardship affected almost every family. Many were "on the Parish", men scavenged for coal on the spoil heaps on the mountainside and everyone tried to maintain human dignity against overwhelming odds.

By early December the drift back to work became a stampede, and when the Miners' Union officially called off the strike, men signed on in their hundreds, daily, in Treharris. The strike was a glorious failure; the men, whose slogan had been "Not a penny off the pay, not a second on the day" returned to work on the Owners' terms with less pay and longer working hours. Thus ended the "single most important event in the industrial history of Great Britain in the 20th Century." (12).

There were many bitter and sad consequences, and the scars were to remain for very many years. One significant event speaks volumes: the Treharris Workmen's Fund had raised £268 for the establishment of a Technical College in Merthyr. The money was used, instead, to relieve the considerable local distress caused by the strike.

Although Deep Navigation remained the main employer in Treharris for the next two decades industrial relations were never amicable.

Social and cultural life of the community, however, flourished in these years. The far-from affluent society of Treharris engaged in a wide -ranging programme of activities. These included sports such as angling, bowls, cycling, football, tennis and a miners' road race. There were church bazaars, flower shows and many musical events. Choral concerts and Cymanfaoedd were very popular and many competitors tested their talents at local and National Eisteddfodau. Educational achievements became increasingly valued.

Many of these activities were faithfully recorded in *The Ocean and National Gazette*. A special section dealt specifically with events at Deep Navigation recording accidents (which were comparatively rare, Deep Navigation having a very good safety record), weddings of miners, births, retirements and deaths. The jewels in the crown were the Ambulance Brigade and the Boys' Club, both strongly associated with the Colliery.

A selection of extracts from the *Ocean and National Gazette* will illustrate the community's social and cultural activities:

Congratulations to the members of our Ambulance Brigade who have again added to their long list of successes. At Porth, on Easter Tuesday, they were successful in winning the cup in the open competition. (1928)

The Boys' Club team were successful in the replayed semi-final match with Abercynon who were defeated by three goals to one. (1928)

Among the names of graduates at the University of Wales, recently published, appear the names of sons and daughters of some of our employees: Wm. Lloyd Williams, Bryn Evans, Miss Enid Morgan, Gwyn Morgan and Ifor Owen. (1928)

Local Bard's success : Our sincere congratulations are extended to Mr Thos. Davies ("Ceiriosydd") who took first prize at Amanford annual Eisteddfod with an essay on "Places and Field Names". (1929)

Two splendid performances were given of the Oratorio Elijah by the Brynhyfryd Welsh Baptist Church on Christmas night and Boxing night. (1929)

At the recent ordination service held at Llanwrtyd, one of the candidates was Mr. William Morgan B.A., son of Mr. George Morgan (haulier, South Pit) and Mrs Morgan and a brother of Mr. Clem Morgan (Cwm Cothi District) (1931).

The Treharris Choral and Operatic Society presented the delightful comic opera "The Geisha" at the Palace during the week February 10th to the 15th. A large proportion of the male members are employed at Deep Navigation

It is our pleasure to place on record the further honour conferred upon Mr D. Roger Jones who at the National Eisteddfod at Llanelli was initiated into the Gorsedd with the title "Dewi Bencerdd." (1930)
During the tour of South Wales by Prince George, Treharris was included in the list of places He visited, He paid a visit to the Boys' Club . A guard of honour was formed by members of the Treharris Ambulance Division. (1932)

Gymanfa.-The annual singing festival of the North Glamorgan Welsh Baptists was held on Whit-Monday at Brynhyfryd, Treharris under the conductorship of Professor Jacob Gabriel, Hengoed. (1934)

International Honour.- The news of the inclusion of Iorwerth Evans in the international rugby fifteen to meet Scotland at Edinburgh was received in the district with much delight. Leaving Caerleon College he became a member of the staff of Bedford School and played for the Bedford rugby team, later joining the London Welsh, for whom he still plays.
This is the first occasion that a local born lad has been selected to represent Wales in the rugby code. (1934)

In many ways it could be said that Deep Navigation served as a focus for the wide-ranging cultural activities of the community, as the Magazine cuttings testify.
With the establishment of Quakers' Yard Secondary School in Edwardsville a new era of educational opportunity dawned in the Valleys. Thirteen Army huts were purchased for £1300 and brought from Salisbury Plain. This "temporary" structure received its first pupils in January, 1922, and the school continued to play a profound role until it was replaced, forty six years later by Afon Taf High School, Troedyrhiw.
No longer were the sons of miners inevitably drawn to be miners themselves. Many local sons and daughters could now envisage careers in a very diverse range of occupations. College and Higher Education beckoned and many Treharris youngsters seized their opportunities. The social order was changing.
These changes were accelerated with the outbreak of war in 1939.
The Ministry of Labour and National Service had been given considerable power to control and direct all available labour to "essential" wartime work. The unemployment of the 1930's was to be almost eliminated during the war years. The nearby Treforest Trading Estate (which had been opened in 1938 as a consequence of the Special Areas Acts) had its 24 factories requisitioned by the Ministry of Aircraft Production. The female population of Treharris was quick to take advantage of the employment opportunities in these and other factories. Many, for the first time, were able to undertake full-time work and thereby add to the weekly wage packets of their families. The Essential Work Order of 1941 tied miners to their "reserved occupation" which prevented them from enlisting in the forces and, also, from entering local munitions factories where working conditions and wages were very attractive. In 1943 Ernest Bevin ordered that one in ten eighteen year old men should be directed to work in the coal industry (as "Bevin boys.").

The female population had no restrictions and could join the forces or take up employment in local factories. In addition to work on the Treforest Estate, Treharris wives, sisters and daughters could find employment further up the Valley in Kayser Bondor, I.C.I., Hall Telephones and Welsh Products Ltd. This economic "emancipation" was to be coupled with social changes to the female life style.

Treharris, in common with many South Wales communities, was to receive an influx of evacuees during the war years. Some of those from London were from the poorer areas of the Capital, whilst the schoolgirls who arrived from Kent were from a more affluent background. An entire girls' school from Folkestone shared the facilities at Quakers' Yard Secondary School for a while.

In many cases the mothers of the evacuee children came to Treharris, bringing with them attitudes and values which were unfamiliar to the locals. The visitors followed their normal practice of relaxing in local public houses in the evenings and at week-ends. This was, initially, quite a shock to the "natives"—particularly to the females. "They are teaching local women to drink" was one response. (13).

It is interesting to reflect on the way people's attitudes, values and beliefs can be challenged and accommodated within a community. Treharris was never quite the same after the evacuee experience!!

Despite the changes there is no doubt that the war brought a closeness and resolve to the people of Treharris. The womenfolk had to cope with rationing and were always on the look-out for treats in the local shops to supplement the family meals. The news that there were "tinned peaches in Lipton's" evoked a rapid response from local housewives! The black-out, sirens, ration books and queues were facts of life but they all added up to a solidarity and common purpose within the community.

The ending of hostilities in 1945 ushered in changes to the economic life of the town. Whilst the manpower employed in Deep Navigation was over 1500, opportunities opened up for both men and women outside of Treharris. The factories at Treforest reverted to peace-time production whilst the large firms which came to Merthyr included Teddington Aircraft Controls, Hoover Ltd., B.S.A., Lines Bros. and Thorn Electrical Industries.

Nevertheless, Deep Navigation remained one of the most highly productive and successful Pits in the South Wales coalfield, with its steam coal in great demand.

Major changes were to have their effect in the next two years.

After over 60 years of private ownership, Deep Navigation Colliery was nationalised in 1947. The following notice was displayed at the Pit :

THIS COLLIERY IS NOW
MANAGED BY THE
NATIONAL
COAL BOARD
ON BEHALF OF THE PEOPLE

Prime Minister Clement Atlee wrote: "The coal mines now belong to the nation. This act offers great possibilities of social advance for the workers, and indeed the whole nation." (14)

Will Lawther, President of the National Union of Mine-workers sent a message to his Union members: " January 1st, 1947, marks the beginning of a new era in the mining industry of Great Britain. We have now left behind the bad old days...." (15)

Mr D.G. Phillips, a retired miner from Treharris, offered the following perspective in an article published in the fifth Annual Report of the South Wales Miners' Library, August 1978- July 1979: "Nationalisation was the miners' dream. He believed it would iron out most of his problems. Before then, the pit was much of a family concern, sons followed father, and everyone knew each other. The manager was a strict fatherly figure, and was very important in the life of the village.

One of the first things the National Coal Board did, was to move all their bosses around. That was the beginning of strangers coming to the pit.. The N.C.B. is such a big concern it lacks the human touch, which I believe to be a great weakness."

Mr Phillips wrote from 48 years' experience at Deep Navigation (1930—1978) and had direct knowledge of the inevitable bureaucracy, which accompanied Nationalisation. Overall, his judgement was that "Nationalisation has done plenty of good. The biggest advantage has been full employment. Another good thing was, they gave the mines a big face-lift. They had run down so badly. All in all, nationalisation has done good for mining."

There is no doubt that, overall, Nationalisation was warmly welcomed by the mining communities of Britain. The close association of the NUM and the NCB under a Labour Government brought high hopes of improved pay and working conditions in the mines. Hard bargaining certainly achieved a great deal for the miners, but it did not eliminate industrial disputes, which were to be ever- present in the years ahead.

Full employment at Deep Navigation and, also, at the many factories in the vicinity brought a new-found financial security to the town and community life benefited greatly. Commercial activities flourished further with a wide range of shops providing a valuable service to the Treharris inhabitants.

The Ocean Players and the Treharris Dramatic Society in the late 1940's and early 50's were among the most successful drama societies in South Wales. Treharris Hall (The Palace) was the venue for a full programme of films and popular concerts. Treharris Athletic Football Club, having been one of the founder members of the Welsh League, first won the South Wales and Monmouth Cup in 1891-2. It remained a prominent member of the Welsh League , playing its home matches on the pitch overlooked by the Commercial Hotel.

Churches continued to play an active part in the life of the town with a number of the chapels hosting annual Cymanfaoedd. Brynhyfryd Welsh Baptist Chapel, for example, was the focus every Whit Monday for the Baptists from the nearby villages who spent the whole day singing hymns and items from Oratorios.

Quakers' Yard Grammar School (formerly Quakers' Yard Municipal Secondary School) continued to provide a valuable gateway to academic success. More local students entered Higher Education and the professions. School teachers became a valuable export.

The Treharris Boys' Club, founded in 1923, was by now one of the most well-known and successful youth organisations in South Wales. Its club house was located within the colliery boundary and benefited from regular contributions from the miners of Deep Navigation.

In the early 1960's Deep Navigation received a £500,000 investment from the NCB. The re-organisation of the colliery involved the installation of 1,540 hp electric winders. Later, skip winding was installed.

By 1960 manpower at Deep Navigation had dropped from the 1935 peak of 2,238 to 1,141 with an output of 327,000 tons.

Part of each miner's remuneration was an entitlement to free loads of coal

Interestingly, despite the huge financial improvements to the colliery, the miners' free coal continued to be delivered in an antiquated way. Each load of coal was delivered by lorry and literally dumped on the pavement and roadway outside the miner's home. The miner - and sometimes his wife – would then have the task of carrying the coal into the house's coal shed for storage.

Coal delivery in Cilhaul, 1972.

The creation of tips of colliery waste as well as the constant movement of trucks of coal created a continuing source of irritation for Treharris housewives. Keeping houses and household washing clear of contamination by coal dust was a never-ending struggle.

This was a domestic irritation shared by all the South Wales mining communities, but the nearby village of Aberfan was to face a catastrophic consequence of coal tipping. On October 21st, 1966, Pantglas Junior School was engulfed in the tip slide which killed 116 children and 28 adults. All the Valley Communities were shaken and a great outcry arose to eliminate the menace of coal tips throughout South Wales. Treharris residents joined in the task of creating a safer environment by eliminating this major problem.

Coal dust, however, remained an unsolved problem in Treharris. Deep Navigation was surrounded on three sides by houses and the inhabitants suffered greatly from this proximity. Huge British Rail diesel locomotives transported waste coal dust from the Pit at night to the Nelson Bog site. This led Mrs Olive Williams who lived almost next to the line to remark, "The house is shaken to its foundations when these locomotives pass. The noise is deafening. They come past late at night and in the early hours of the morning carrying as many as 30 loaded trucks behind them."(16)

Heavy lorries taking coal to the blending site at the colliery were also blamed for the town's noise and dust problems. Local resident Mrs Kay Jones complained that "the paintwork (in her home) is thick with coal dust and there's no point in washing the windows. The black dust finds its way into the kitchen at the back of the house and I am dreading the fine weather." (17)

Residents of Bontnewydd Terrace presented a petition to the Merthyr Council's Environmental Health Department who promised to monitor the nuisance. The NCB promised to try to solve the problem.

As the Centenary of Deep Navigation approached, ominous storm clouds were gathering in Central Government. The Conservatives had been defeated at the hands of the mineworkers in 1972 and 1974. Contingency planning at the very highest level was to take place in anticipation of future strikes by mineworkers. Out of these deliberations emerged the 'Ridley Plan.' Nicholas Ridley was the chairman of an influential group of Conservative back-benchers charged with the task of drawing up a series of proposals for the nationalised industries. It called for vigorous denationalisation. In the annexe to the Plan Ridley, anticipating a 'political threat' from the Labour movement, regarded the coalfields as the most likely battlefield. Accordingly, in anticipation of a future coal strike, the Ridley group believed that a government should (a) build up maximum coal stocks, particularly at the power stations; (b) make contingency plans for the import of coal; (c) encourage the recruitment of non-union drivers by haulage companies to help move coal when necessary; and (d) introduce dual coal/oil firing in the power stations.

Whilst the Ridley Plan, at the time, seemed to disappear without trace, it was to prove a cornerstone of clandestine Conservative policy in the days ahead and was to prove decisive in the Strike of 1984/5.

As Deep Navigation prepared to celebrate its Centenary in 1979 no one could have imagined that in twelve years' time the Pit would fall victim to the Government's Pit Closure Programme.

But 1979 was party time in Treharris and the whole town joined in the Centenary festivities. More than 2,000 people attended a celebration party at the Pit, with trips to the bottom of the colliery proving a major attraction for relatives of the 780 miners. There were balloon races, a brass band concert, a road race, and surprise presents. Many congratulatory telegrams were received.

A commemorative medal was struck which was presented to all workers at Deep Navigation Colliery. On one side of the medal was depicted a crouching miner of 100 years ago complete with cap and pick-axe. His modern-day counterpart was figured on the other side.

After 100 years the colliery's future seemed assured. The mine was judged to be " one of our very best collieries" by a National Coal Board spokesman. He added, "It produces 2.74 tonnes per man per week —double the average for South Wales and better than the national average."(18).

Most of the 8,500 tonnes of coal produced per week was earmarked for Aberthaw Power Station, with 30 per cent going for industrial use.

Postcard of the Colliery on sale in the town.

A few years later, in 1982, there was cause for more optimism regarding Deep Navigation's future when a brand new canteen to accommodate 100 people was erected at the colliery. Made of pre-fabricated colour-coated steel, the air-conditioned building cost £70,000 with £23,000 worth of kitchen equipment. As well as eating space and cooking facilities the new block contained offices and toilets.

A year later there was even more heartening news. More than £6 million was allocated to Deep Navigation for the installation of new equipment at the colliery. Mr Cliff Davies, the National Coal Board's South Wales area Deputy (mining), announced, "Deep Navigation has proved itself to be one of the best mines in Wales. It has established an unparalleled record for success—and the mining industry can afford to invest only in successful pits." (19).

A £3million high-speed push-button system for raising coal was installed enabling coal to be raised 100 tonnes an hour faster than the existing maximum. The output from number one shaft face was expected to be around 1,500 tonnes a day. The pit reserves were estimated to be in the region of 11 million tons. Yes, the future looked very rosy.

Early in 1984 the intention was to mine the previously untouched Gellideg seams, 2,500 feet below ground where, it was estimated, sufficient coal existed to keep the Treharris miners busy for 20 years. The face was to be worked by a revolutionary double-ended shearer which saved time and enabled the coal to be transported to the surface by an automatic rapid skip winding system. Manager Mr Brian Preece said,

"We are on the threshold of the most exciting period of the colliery's modern history. This is our face for the future." (20).
Seven years later the mine was closed.

Deep Navigation and the entire coal industry in Britain were, in fact, on the threshold of one of the most bitter industrial disputes in the country's history. The miners' strike of 1984/5 was to mark the beginning of the end for many of Britain's coal mines— including Deep Navigation, Treharris.
The high hopes for the industry following nationalisation seemed justified when the NCB and the NUM developed a new and productive relationship. The aim of the NUM at that time was to attain joint authority over the industry together with the NCB . Co-operation and hard bargaining marked the early years of the new arrangement.
For the next thirty years a new consensus developed in which a post-war bargain prevailed between organised labour and the establishment.
However, progressively, the core issue centred on the NCB's right to manage.
When Mrs Thatcher succeeded Ted Heath as Conservative leader in 1975, she was keenly aware of the effect of the miners' strike of 1972 which had smashed the government's pay policy and then, in 1974, had forced the election which brought down the Heath government. Margaret Thatcher's new style Conservatism "saw in the Coal Board and its supposedly cosy relationship with the NUM a paradigm of the soft feather-bedding and acceptance of enormous subsidy which it believed had destroyed Britain's economic prospects." (21)
It was clear that this "cosy relationship" was about to cease. In 1980 the Conservative government declared that by 1983-4 all operating grants given to the NCB would be ended. From then on the Board would have to make a profit.
Soon, the battle lines were drawn.
On to the National stage entered the key protagonists Ian McGregor Chairman of the NCB, and Arthur Scargill, President of the NUM.
The details of the strike called in 1984 are well-documented. Suffice to say that great bitterness prevailed throughout the period of the strike. Scargill's insistence that the strike could be called without a national ballot, the tactic of militant picketing and the use of very large contingents of police all contributed to the national unease.
At local as well as national level considerable economic hardship affected miners and their families. Great controversy raged over the DHSS's payment of supplementary benefit. A spokesman for the DHSS in Merthyr explained the policy in these terms : "We pay the striker for his wife and children, not the striker himself, and from regulations introduced in 1980 we have to deduct £15 strike pay, irrespective of whether the striker concerned is receiving any strike pay. For example, a married couple would get £43.45 supplementary benefit. A trades dispute man gets £21.45 for his wife and there are rates for the children depending on age and circumstances." (22)
Not surprisingly, household bills for rent, electricity, gas and water soon fell into arrears. The respective providers, to their credit, adopted a sympathetic approach to the plight of the striking miners. The authorities' view was summarised in the following way : "We look at cases on a personal basis and try to reach an agreement where the

customer pays what he feels he can afford. The budget scheme where payment is spread evenly through the year is popular." (23).

Shopkeepers and tradesmen throughout the Borough were soon affected by the lack of buying power of the striking miners and their families.

A Trelewis shopkeeper reported, " The strike is affecting trade. I will never recover the lost money. Food items are selling - but slowly; most affected is the sweets, ice-cream and pop." (24).

At Imperial Bakery, Abercynon the cost of white sliced loaves was reduced to 28p for the duration of the strike. This was a considerable saving to miners, but it also meant a considerable cut in the Company's profit margin.

A Trelewis newsagent and tobacconist received a triple blow. The lady owner reported, "Trade is down, and with my husband and son both miners, there is no money apart from the wages from the shop." (25).

In the autumn coal stocks began to dwindle and this threatened a number of schools in the Borough. Ten schools faced imminent closure, with 2,000 children in danger of being sent home – a direct effect of the lack of heating due to inadequate coal stocks.

Although miners were on strike they were not idle. Scargill's strategy of mass picketing put pressure on all miners to be pro-active . Merthyr Vale miners travelled to Oxford where they received substantial support from a range of groups and organisations. The Oxford Support Group raised £111,000 in cash and food for the miners. After visits to Cannock Chase coalfields and other pits, the Merthyr Vale miners were asked to picket Didcot power station. One unexpected outcome of the time spent in Oxford by the Merthyr Vale miners took the form of two marriages between the visiting miners and two local women.

Treharris miners were allotted a very different picketing task which took them to Exmouth, my home for 40 years. In 1984 Exmouth Docks was an active port for many cargo ships.

Four weeks after the strike had started, a sharp-eyed Labour supporter noticed that three ships laden with coal from the Continent were being unloaded. The chairman of the Exmouth Docks Company admitted that 16 more ships were shortly due to arrive. The cargo was anthracite for non-industrial use in the Westcountry.

Mr Ray Davison, Secretary of Exmouth Labour Party, was alerted to this situation and the NUM was informed. The official response was to ask the docks manager to stop the unloading—or else the South Wales miners would be asked to picket the docks.

The unloading continued.

In early April the first miners' pickets arrived and persuaded the dockers to "black" a ship carrying a 900-ton cargo of Polish coal. Within the next few months over 100 miners arrived in Exmouth and were received by the local Labour Party's Miners' Support Group led by the charismatic activist Ray Davison. He was to prove pivotal in organising support for the visiting miners. In late summer he and his team regularly travelled to Treharris to deliver food, clothing, footwear, fresh vegetables and money to Deep Navigation miners and their families. The *Exmouth Herald* at the end of September published an article and a picture of Mr Davison carrying a Cheddar cheese weighing over half-a-hundredweight. This was a gift from a famous Devon farm - Quick's of Newton St Cyres.

A number of meetings were arranged in the months up to Christmas '84 when small groups of Treharris miners attended to explain their action and to answer questions posed by the general public. As Christmas approached various events were organised and vanloads of toys and food left Exmouth for Treharris.

Applications to hold Street Collections in Sidmouth and Exmouth to aid the Treharris miners were refused by the District and local Councils. (It should be noted that East Devon is regarded as a Tory stronghold). A second request was made in the early part of 1985; Exmouth Town Council, again, refused permission.

In South Wales there was a slow drift back to work . Inevitably, the writing was on the wall; the Strike would soon be over.

The South Wales NUM decided to return to work 'en masse.'

But the Treharris miners didn't forget the friends who had supported them in their struggle. More than forty members of the East Devon Miners' Support Group were invited to visit Treharris and the Deep Navigation Pit in May 1985. Lunch was provided at the Boys' Club, which had served as a soup kitchen during the strike. The visitors were then given a guided tour of the upper areas of the pit and later visited Aberfan to pay respect to those who died in the 1965 Disaster. Local miners then entertained the group at the pithead club. Local miners' President, Dickie Tanner, paid tribute to the work of the East Devon Miners' Support Group and its organiser, Ray Davison. The visitors responded by presenting a cheque for £1,000 and a specially commissioned hand carved wooden plaque to Lyn Roberts, Treharris Lodge Chairman, as a momento of the bonds forged between East Devon and the pit village.

In December 1985, the links were again strengthened when representatives of the East Devon Miners' Support Group travelled to Treharris to deliver five Christmas cakes for the children of pit workers at their Christmas parties.

Six months after the strike was over, Ray Davison and the Exmouth Miners' Support Group lodged a complaint to the Ombudsman over the behaviour of East Devon District Council in refusing Street Collections on behalf of the striking miners. In August, 1986 the Ombudsman rejected the complaint. In his conclusion he stated, "The Support Group claims political bias. There may have been but that is not unusual. " (26). A remarkable admission, indeed!

Over the ensuing years Exmouth became a favoured holiday destination for Treharris families when old friendships were renewed. In November 1988, forty Welsh miners and their wives returned to Exmouth to honour an Exmouth Labour Party stalwart, Norah Stuart. A presentation of a merit award for "outstanding voluntary service" was made to Norah by Alan Burt, Chair of the Deep Navigation NUM Lodge. Norah also received a copper engraving of Treharris and a bronze and oak model of a pit head.

Deep Navigation Pit was, at this stage, working normally and there was a limited sense of optimism following the £2 million cash injection in 1986 from British Coal. The overall output per manshift had risen from 3.10 tonnes to 3.94 and management was confident that a return to profitable mining would soon be a reality.

In 1987 production at Deep Navigation was at a standstill as miners voted to strike over a new high technology coal face.

By the time the miners returned to work British Coal claimed a loss of £140,000 as a result of the strike. Later in the same year and despite the massive monetary investment in the Pit, Deep Navigation was failing to meet its production target. The mine's output was 8,000 tonnes of coal a week - a shortfall of 5,000 tonnes. Warnings were given that the Pit would have to get back to profit. Yet in November 700 Deep Navigation workers called a strike after a row over seniority at the Pit.

The week-long dispute ended after NUM officials warned the workers they were jeopardising the Pit's future by remaining on strike. British Coal's Area Director welcomed the decision but attacked the loss of 100,000 tonnes of coal output when the mine was struggling to become viable.

By 1990 more storm clouds were gathering as the issue of Pit closures remained high on the political agenda. Uneconomic pits were a prime target and the outlook for Deep Navigation was not encouraging. British Coal estimated that the Pit was only producing 37 per cent of its target. A high-ranking British Coal official said that the financial results for the December (1989) quarter were very poor and that he was not satisfied with the performance of Deep Navigation.

In March 1990 British Coal made the decision not to close the Colliery. This was to prove a false dawn, but at the time the news was greeted with great relief.

By August British Coal reported that the Pit was achieving over and above its target and the 570 jobs at the Colliery were safe. The Lodge Secretary at Deep Navigation said, "The pit has made a profit of £1m in the first four months of the year and we have been given an assurance that as long as we are making a profit our jobs are safe. Morale at the pit is good at the moment and production levels are excellent."

Morale at the nearby village of Edwardsville was not high, however. The residents were complaining that their homes were being damaged by subsidence as a result of mining at the Colliery. As discussions with British Coal were under way, rumours were circulating regarding the impending closure of Deep Navigation.

British Coal released an estimate of coal reserves at Deep Navigation; these reserves were expected to run out by 1994. An informed source stated that closure could come sooner.

The writing was on the wall.

Finally the announcement came that Deep Navigation would cease production on March 29 (Good Friday) 1991. Immediately, there were plans by the Treharris population to mark the end of an era in a dignified and appropriate way. On the Sunday before Good Friday the Colliery opened its doors to the public. More than 1,000 people turned out to tour the Pit and to experience trips down the mine.

Special plates were produced and an order placed for inscribed miners' lamps as farewell gifts to the workforce

To commemorate the final closure there were remarkable scenes in the town. These were described in a *"Merthyr Express"* article as follows :

"120 years of mining history paraded through the streets of Treharris on Good Friday as the village marked the closure of the oldest working mine in Great Britain. Miners, former miners, their families and villagers took to the streets in their thousands to witness the event which closes a chapter in Treharris's history.

The unprecedented parade through the streets was led by the Salvation Army and followed by the miners, still wearing their pit clothes and caked in coal dust, who had completed the last - ever working shift.

Major Porter of the Salvation Army led a service at the pit to commemorate the end and to remember the men who were killed in underground disasters during the mine's history."

Streets were festooned in flags and bunting as the crowds gathered in the Colliery yard and at the Pit gates for a final blaze of glory. The NUM banner was paraded in the Colliery yard, through Fox Street, followed by a procession. One placard proclaimed "Don't Worry; Be Happy"

Members of Treharris Boys' Club turned out in force to demonstrate their gratitude to the miners for their unrivalled support over many years.

Also present was a delegation from East Devon Support Group who had, earlier, been given a tour of the pit bottom and had been specially invited to attend a party at the Boys' Club. Thus ended the celebration of the history of the Pit which had been the economic main-stay of Treharris for over 100 years.

Closure parade for Deep Navigation colliery, Treharris 1991.

In April underground salvage operations were in full swing with a plan to fill in the shaft in May. Demolition continued throughout the summer months though the Washery continued to be operative until the final stocks of coal were exhausted. Then it, too, was dismantled.

Quite soon the realisation dawned that there would, shortly, be no evidence that Deep Navigation ever existed.

But the spirit of Treharris people couldn't be extinguished that easily.

Soon plans were drawn up to create sporting and other facilities on the old Pit site. The Taff Bargoed Development Trust was established and soon attracted grants of £500,000 from the Welsh Office as part of a Community Revival Strategy.

The old Pit site was landscaped & incorporated a sports' field. The Millennium Park was created and this has become the venue of the Treharris Festival held at the end of June each year. The Festival starts in the town with a procession led by the Treharris NUM Lodge Banner. The marchers end up in the Millennium Park where bands play and there is a host of children's entertainments.

Other Agencies combined to produce the Taff Bargoed Community Park in nearby Nelson/ Bedlinog. Here is sited an Indoor Sports' Centre and the Welsh International Climbing Wall - one of the largest indoor climbing walls in the United Kingdom.

Nearby a series of cascades and reed beds have been formed which have greatly enhanced the environmental attraction of the area.

So, real progress has been made on many fronts. There have been casualties, of course. Sadly, no agreement was reached over other potential uses for the Palace which had been a very popular cinema and venue for concerts. The Palace was completely demolished and there is now no evidence that it was once the entertainments centre of the town.

The Treharris Boys' Club is also facing an uncertain future having been, for many years, the jewel in the crown of community provision for young people.

The sub-title of this article is "The Story of a Pit and its Town."

There is nothing more to be said about the Pit. It has gone.

The town, however, remains and its people have to face up to a future as uncertain as any in the history of the place. They are left to reflect on the achievements of their forebears and draw comfort from the resilience of the people who created the vibrant, industrious community of Treharris.

From its earliest beginnings the people sought to establish a caring and successful town. Houses were built, chapels and churches established and shops and offices created to meet the needs of the expanding population.

It became an enterprising town with a wide range of cultural activities. Music and drama predominated side by side with sporting endeavours.

There is a very great deal to be proud of as one reflects on the history of Treharris.

But, what if the town had never come into existence? What if the verdant pastures at the lower end of the Merthyr valley had remained untouched by the industrial revolution?

What if Mr Harris had never visited the area?

Again, this is idle speculation.

With immense gratitude we can make the judgement that if it hadn't been for Mr Harris, then a wonderful community might never have been created.

Yes, indeed…………………..if it hadn't been for Mr Harris……..

Acknowledgements :

First and foremost my thanks go to my elder son Lyn for allowing me to use the wealth of material he collected whilst researching the history of Treharris Pit for a school Project.

My thanks go, too, to Dr Fred Holley who provided me with invaluable data as a result of his untiring efforts in examining the Merthyr Express archives at Merthyr Central Library.

Details of the picketing of Exmouth Docks by Treharris miners and of the work of the East Devon Support Group For The Miners was readily provided by Ray Davison to whom I express my sincere gratitude.

I am also grateful to the following:

Mr Alun Williams of Nelson for allowing use of the photograph of the Huts & of his son, Peter.

Logaston Press: for the photo reproduced by permission of Martin Dunkerton from "Is It Still Raining In Aberfan ?" (Logaston Press) now out of print.

Merthyr Tydfil Public Libraries for permitting use of photographs from their 1998 Heritage Calendar and also from "Valley Views" Book 4.

References:

The Miners' Strike: M. Adeney & J. Lloyd . Routledge & Kegan Paul
The People of Wales: ed G.E. Jones and D. Smith. Gomer
Is It Still Raining In Aberfan? M. Doel & M. Dunkerton .Logaston Press 1991
The Historic Taf Valleys. Volume Two: J. Perkins, J. Evans & M. Gillham 1982.
Merthyr Historian Vol. Ten. Merthyr Tydfil Historical Society 1999
Merthyr Tydfil- A Valley Community. Merthyr Teachers' Centre Group 1981
Valley Views Book 4: Coal Mining in Merthyr Tydfil & District
Merthyr Tydfil Heritage Calendar 1998. Merthyr Tydfil Public Libraries Leisure Services Department.

Quotation Sources :

1,3 and 4 The Merthyr Historian Volume 14. "Sinking Harris's Navigation Collieries" T.F. Holley.
2   Mrs C.E. Williams pers. com.
5 and 6, 9 and 10. Letters written by Mrs Mary Jenkins to her emigrant sons from copies provided by Mr Geraint Rees of the Sydney Welsh Society, Australia.
7 The Express, Oct 3rd 1936.
8 Advertisement in The Ocean and National Gazette
11 Copy of letter written by Lenin to Thomas Bell.
12 Merthyr Historian Volume 2
13 The People of Wales ed. G.E. Jones and D. Smith
14 and 15 NCB pamphlet "Vesting Day January 1st, 1947"
16 and 17 Merthyr Express reports
18 Merthyr Express .
19 Merthyr Express 29.08 .1983.
20 Merthyr Express 9.01.1984
21   The Miners' Strike: M. Adeney & J. Lloyd . Routledge & Kegan Paul
22, 23, 24 and 25. Merthyr Express 5.07.1984.
26 Exmouth Herald 29.08.1986

DISTURBANCES IN WALES: A LETTER FROM MERTHYR, 20th. OCTOBER 1816
by
INNES MACLEOD

On the 3rd. of February 1852 Mr. Henry Austin Bruce, who sat as a magistrate in the Merthyr Tydfil Police Court, gave a talk in the Bush Inn to the local Young Men's Mutual Improvement Society on *Merthyr in 1852*. Bruce began by contrasting the preservation of peace and good order in Merthyr Tydfil in 1852 by a police force of eighteen men dressed in blue and armed with bits of sticks, with the difficulties the authorities had in coping with the dangerous indiscipline and savagery of the riots in 1816 and 1831: these events, he knew, had remained 'fresh in the memory of their neighbours' and had made 'the very name of Merthyr a sound of terror in their eye' (1). This was, of course, scarcely an impartial or adequate interpretation of how the disturbances of 1816 and 1831 were remembered at that time, and other commentators might, no doubt, have preferred to emphasise their importance, both locally and nationally, as part of the long struggle for freedom and justice. Bruce was, however, correct in seeing the events of 1816 as being in scale and nature comparable with the much better known riots in 1831.

The disturbances in the Valleys, in Merthyr Tydfil, Dowlais, Tredegar, Ebbw Vale, Sirhowy, Nantyglo, Blaenavon, Pontypool, Abergavenny and Llanelly, and also in Brecon in October 1816 were essentially a popular reaction to problems stemming from a general post-war, post-1815 economic depression, and in particular to the imposition of reductions in wage levels, to the threat and / or reality of job losses, and to specific local problems and injustices, for example the system of trucking used by some companies. Hundreds and indeed thousands of men, colliers, miners, puddlers, withdrew their labour; some moved towards Merthyr Tydfil in a mass protest movement; many took direct industrial action in closing down iron works and furnaces, and even threatening to destroy the mills supplying the company shops in the hills with flour.

The disturbances in Glamorgan and Monmouthshire, and in Birmingham, Manchester, Glasgow, Sheffield, etc., were variously reported in metropolitan London newspapers and in local provincial newspapers throughout Britain. By 1810 most of the larger towns, Bristol, Bath, Hereford, Swansea, Carlisle, Salisbury, Gloucester, Chester, Glasgow, Aberdeen, Dumfries, had a 'local' newspaper; some, for example, Bristol and Dumfries, had two competing weekly journals. These were not 'local' newspapers in the modern sense of the word. Their columns were largely filled up with reports copied or plagiarised, occasionally with but often without any acknowledgement, from London daily and weekly papers, for example *The Gentleman's Magazine,* and other provincial journals. Colin Munro, publisher of the *Dumfries and Galloway Courier*, which was founded in 1809 and had, by 1814, a circulation of about 1,035 copies, was also the proprietor of the 'London Newspaper Office' in Dumfries. It supplied in Dumfries and Galloway fifteen London daily papers, *The British Press, Times, Post, Pilot, Herald, Advertiser, Ledger, Globe, Statesman, Sun, Day, Traveller, Chronicle, Courier,* and *Star,* and also probably   carried some provincial papers, for example *The Bristol Mirror* and *The Bristol Herald, The Manchester Mercury* and *The Birmingham Herald.* (2).

The *Dumfries and Galloway Courier,* and its rival, the older *Dumfries Weekly Journal,* founded by Robert Jackson in 1777, filled up their columns in 1816 with a vast inchoate miscellany of reports from Ballinasloe and Londonderry in Ireland, from Chester Assizes and the Shadwell Police Office in London, from Georgia, from Haiti, from the Cape Coast Castle in West Africa, etc.. Their contents might have been taken from *The Times, The London Gazette, The Dundee and Cupar Advertiser, The Kentish Gazette,* and indeed from any one or other of between 150 and 200 newspapers.

The *Dumfries Weekly Journal* of 29th. October 1816 included extracts from a letter sent from Merthyr Tydfil and dated for Sunday 20th. October, and this was followed by a more general and brief assessment of the continuing situation in Merthyr and in Brecon. The letter **may** have been taken from a provincial newspaper published in England or Wales. (It was not copied from the superficially most obvious candidate, *The Cambrian,* published in Swansea). It does, however, seem more likely that the letter was sent directly from Merthyr by a successful businessman, perhaps a Scotch draper and tea dealer, to a son or daughter living in Dumfries and Galloway and was then passed on to Robert Jackson. Note the personal details. Were the 'several' others in the house (in addition to 'your mother') young apprentice travelling drapers and tea dealers? The writer was able to give away a very substantial two pounds sterling worth of freshly baked bread plus cheese. He dealt tactfully and wisely with the crowd arriving en masse in Merthyr, offering good advice, sympathy and sustenance. The specific details on stopping the furnaces and works is very interesting.

DISTURBANCES IN WALES. MERTHYR, SUNDAY 20.10.1816. TEXT OF THE LETTER.

"On Wednesday last about 400 men rose from their work at Tredegar ironworks; they came on to Rumney works, and put the blast out from the furnaces, and pressed several men to go along to the Dowlais works, where they did the same: also at Penydavron (Penydarren), they stopped all the furnaces on the hills (their plea was advance of wages): the mob passed by Pontmorlais to Cyfarthfa ironworks, and stopped all the blast furnaces and most of the works: they pressed many of the workers to go along with them.

On Wednesday evening their numbers were increasing to many hundreds, if not thousands. They got to the Plymouth works, and stopped them all. In the evening, after stopping all the works in the neighbourhood, the men came into the town of Merthyr in a large body, perhaps many thousands, some with sticks, and others with pikes and other weapons in their hands. There was a very large crowd, and several of the men knocked at my door about 10 o'clock on Wednesday evening; your mother, myself, and several were in my house; all the lights, except a little fire, were put out, but we had prepared for the worst; we had plenty of candles, etc., in readiness; however, the men knocked furiously at my front door. I opened it, and asked what they wanted: their answer was, 'bread and cheese'.

I told them to behave peaceable, and I would give all the bread and cheese in the house among them. One fellow with a large hay-fork in his hand, stepped up to my door, and swore they would not injure any thing, so they had all my bread and cheese, as they wanted victuals. Very fortunately we had been baking that day, partly on purpose, as I had seen their manoeuvres in several places about. However, your mother and all in my house lent a hand to cut and serve out the bread and cheese, while myself and others were reasoning with the men, and making use of the best and most persuasive means we could. In the course of half an hour they all gave a general huzza! and went away to other parts of the town where they could get victuals. The mob has not done any more injury than stopping all the works. I gave away, perhaps, about £2 worth of bread and cheese.

Dispatches were sent to different parts for military. Mr. Forrest travelled all Wednesday night for Bristol, others to Cardiff, Swansea. Three stage coaches were pressed at Cardiff, which were loaded full in and outside with soldiers. They reached Merthyr on Friday morning.

They (the rioters) went over the hills to Nanty-Gloe, Lanelly, Blane-Avon; and every work on the hills they stopped. They were to return to Merthyr yesterday (Saturday) about two o'clock. They arrived in a body supposed to be at least 10, 000. About half an hour before the mob, the Bristol soldiers (part of the 55th. regiment) came in; they had scarcely time to have a cup of beer and a little bread in their hands at the Castle Inn (headquarters) before the mob came in in thousands. Mr. Hill, the Sheriff for Glamorgan, Mr. Crawshay, and all the Gentlemen, mounted their horses with the cavalry. The riot act was read by Mr. Hill, the Sheriff. After great bustle and noise, the mob were all dispersed last evening, without firing or injuring any one by the military. Last evening, after they dispersed, nearly 40 of the ringleaders were made prisoners; to-morrow they will be sent to Cardiff gaol. Had not the mob dispersed when they did, the order to fire would have been given in a few more minutes; had that been the case, the slaughter would have been dreadful, for many of the innocent, who were spectators, would have fallen with others.
P.S. Every thing is quiet at Merthyr this morning; all the military, etc. are gone to the church.

"The latest letters from Merthyr Tydvil are of the 22nd. inst. They state that the rioters continued quiet, and that the military daily increase in numbers. In consequence of a disposition to riot at Brecon, a strong force had been sent to protect the arms deposited there. The military now being in possession of the place, all apprehension for the safety of the arms had ceased.

One class of the workmen at Merthyr, called the Padlers (ie. puddlers), have been induced to return to their work without a compromise; but these are the men who are paid the highest prices. There are four in number employed to each furnace. The colliers and miners, the persons who are paid the lowest wages, are still refractory, and have not returned to their work; but as the different works have a good supply of coal and iron material at hand, their services may be dispensed with for some time to come". (*Dumfries Weekly Journal*. 29.10.1816.)

Jackson, the proprietor and editor of the *Journal* , took a very 'common sense' view of the remedies required to deal with the unrest and distress in industrial areas in Britain. "The only method of allaying these dangerous symptoms is to find immediate means of providing the poor with employment ⋯ perfectly practicable in every part of the country ⋯ to raise money ⋯ very inconsiderable in proportion to the resources of the country and ⋯ provide work for all the unemployed poor during the approaching winter". (3)

The *Dumfries and Galloway Courier* of 29th. October 1816 included only brief reports on the situation in Merthyr and these were clearly taken from other newspapers.

The Riots

"Merthyr-Tydvil, Oct. 20. We are busy here examining the rioters and committing them. All is quiet and not a rioter to be seen; but not a man will work now, mob or no mob - soldiers or no soldiers: they will not even complete their month's notice. We hope they will presently see things in their proper light, and petition us to carry on the work at such wages as we can afford. This is the first point we wish to bring them to.

Memorandum

Two men were killed and several wounded, of the rioters; they were fired upon whilst taking away what is termed the blast from one of the furnaces. Ten shillings is the smallest sum the lowest class of workmen were required to be reduced to per week; others were to have fifteen shillings, and some as high as a guinea. The proprietors allow that the men require more in order to enable them and their families to live; but it is not in their power to give more in the present depreciated state of the iron trade.

Bristol, Oct. 21. I have the satisfaction to assure you that the decisive and vigorous measures taken by the sheriff and magistrates at Merthyr-Tydvil have entirely suppressed the disturbances. As no insult was offered to the troops, not a shot was fired, but the streets of Merthyr were cleared by them, and many of the rioters apprehended without resistance of any sort. They are now in Cardiff gaol; and the furnaces were set to work again. Too much praise cannot be given to the Swansea and Cardiff Yeomanry Cavalry, for the alacrity, steadiness, and temper, they displayed. The magistrates too are entitled to every praise for their decision, judgment, and firmness; and the government in London, it appears, was most prompt and vigorous in ordering such powerful assistance as by its indisputable strength was likely to prevent bloodshed". (4)

For further details of the <u>Disturbances in Glamorganshire</u> and the situation in Merthyr Tydfil on Wednesday, Thursday and Friday, 16th. - 18th. October 1816 see *The Cambrian* for 26th. October.

"On Friday morning last we received the first intimation of a popular commotion at Merthyr and its vicinity ⋯ In consequence of a requisition from the Magistracy, the Swansea Volunteer Cavalry, under the command of Major Hughes, assembled with all possible alacrity, marched from hence about four on Saturday morning, and reached Merthyr at noon, where they joined the Cardiff Cavalry, commanded by Captain Wood; a detachment of the 55th. Infantry from Bristol, consisting of almost one hundred men; and the Staff of the Royal Glamorgan Militia who had to that time kept the mob in awe.

Our Cavalry arrived at the moment a large body of the populace was entering the town, and a general charge was ordered shortly afterwards; but, happily, this was prevented by the misguided men dispersing, of their own accord, and tranquillity prevailed universally before night. Three of the ringleaders were taken into custody and lodged in Cardiff Gaol on Sunday morning; they were escorted hither by the Cardiff Cavalry on their return home. Three others have also been committed, and two women who used most inflammatory language, have been sent to the House of Correction at Cowbridge.

The workmen have been gradually returning to their labour in the Merthyr and other furnaces in the neighbourhood; some of these, however, towards Abergavenny, continued on Wednesday in a refractory state, but order and regulation were expected to be restored yesterday, two troops of the 23rd. Light Dragoons having been dispatched from Bristol by the direction of Lord Sidmouth ⋯

The disposition to riot and disorder originated in a notice given by one of the works in the hills of a further reduction in wages ⋯ Thus circumstanced, the men's wages have been reduced considerably, and in some cases are so low as to cause great distress when the families are numerous. When the above-mentioned notice of a still further reduction was given on Wednesday se'nnight, a numerous body of the men assembled, and in the course of the following two days stopped the work at every furnace in and out of Merthyr, with one exception, we believe, only.

They were ineffectually resisted at Dowlais, on Thursday evening, by some magistrates and gentlemen at the head of some sixty special constables, armed with pikes; the latter were disarmed and dispersed, and four of the former were much hurt by vollies of stones. The windows of Mr. Guest's house were demolished, and the mob paraded the streets at night. After this ⋯ no other mischief was done; the men continued to assemble in numerous groups until the middle of Saturday, when, upon again re-entering the town, they found the military ready to receive them, and the tumult was quelled as already stated ⋯

We cannot doubt of the iron-masters doing all in their power to alleviate the distresses of the workmen, and the latter will find their account in being quiet and orderly ⋯

Some alarm was excited at Pontypool, but it soon subsided. Fears were also entertained for the safety of the depot at Brecon, where there are 40,000 stand of arms, but it is now effectually secured against attack by a detachment of the 55th. from Milford, and the Staff of the Carmarthenshire Militia ····" (5).

In the following week *The Cambrian* included letters from Lord Sidmouth in Whitehall, from Richard Davies in Brecon, from a member of the Cardiff Cavalry describing 'the first charge' at Merthyr Tydfil, and from 'A Friend of Justice' in Abergavenny referring to events in Llanelly, Nantyglo and Blaenavon. The Blaenavon men only wanted that their masters would not curtail their wages further ---- "they would endeavour to go on for what they were paid, provided they should receive the same weekly, and provided they should have permission to lay out the little they earned, with great labour, where and when they pleasure, and not be compelled to purchase what they wanted at the Shop of the Company". (6).

The same issue of *The Cambrian* included a summary of the situation and what turned out to be an accurate prediction of the appropriate punishment of the leaders of the disturbances. "The misguided individuals who were the authors of the excesses, by their early submission to legal authority, and quick return to orderly habits, will, we hope, be considered as having made some small atonement for their recent misconduct; if their future good behaviour shall appear to warrant oblivion of past offences, we think we can venture to assert that this lenity will not be denied to them. But they must bear in mind this important truth, that 'Rioting' never fails to defeat its own object". (7).

The sentences imposed at the Cardiff and the Monmouth Assizes in April 1817 were intended to "serve as a caution for deluded men, how they in future transgress against the laws of their country". At Cardiff Rawlins Haddock was imprisoned for twelve months for rioting at Merthyr Tydfil; Thomas Gwillim received six months; and David Davis and William Llewellin three months. At Monmouth John Evans, for riotous assembly with others at Tredegar Iron-Works and for stopping one of the steam-engines, was imprisoned for twelve months. (8).

References.
(1) Cardiff and Merthyr Guardian, 7th. February 1852.
(2) Dumfries and Galloway Courier, 5th. October 1813 and 11th. January 1814.
(3) Dumfries Weekly Journal, 5th. November 1816.
(4) Dumfries and Galloway Courier, 29th. October 1816.
(5) The Cambrian, 26th. October 1816.
(6) The Cambrian, 2nd. November 1816.
(7) The Cambrian, 2nd. November 1816.
(8) The Cambrian, 12th. April 1817.

GARTH GYNYD HAMLET BEFORE THE COAL PITS
by
JUDITH JONES

The area of Garth Gynyd Hamlet[1] (Bedlinog) is in the Bargoed Taff valley, a tributary of the Taff to the south east of Merthyr Tydfil in northeast Glamorgan. It covered the western side of Cefn Gelligaer ridge down to the Bargoed Taff River, between its tributaries, Nant y Garth in the south and Nant y Ffin in the north (see Map 1) and was centred on the present-day village of Bedlinog. The boundaries of the hamlet were described in a document of 1750 when a group of parishioners walked the boundaries of Gelligaer Parish and its hamlets; those of Garth Gynyd read:

...it begins where Nant y Garth goes to Bargoed Taff then along the river Bargoed Taff until it comes to Nant y Ffeen then along Nant y Ffeen to Fynnon y Garn Ddu then directly to Fose Tor Kenla then along the highway downwards to Pen Ca Ifor then along the way westward to Funon Cluide Trawska then to Nant y Garth opposite Craig Fargoed Meeting House then along Nant y Garth to Bargoed River aforesaid...[2]

It is probable that previous volumes of the *Merthyr Historian* have not included articles about the Garth Gynyd area because, historically, this was part of the parish of Gelligaer. Gelligaer and Merthyr Parishes, however, have been intertwined administratively as far back as the times of the Welsh princes, and throughout the medieval period they formed Uwch Caiach, the northern-most section of the Lordship of Senghenydd. Subsequent local government has also been on a joint basis, such as for Poor Law and Sanitary Districts[3] and in 1973 the Bargoed Taff Valley was incorporated into the Merthyr Tydfil administrative area.

In common with the rest of the South Wales upland area, prior to the development of industry, Garth Gynyd was an agricultural community and it is intended to illustrate how, in just a few decades, this completely rural, almost self-sufficient, society and economy was destroyed and replaced by one dependant on the coal industry. In particular I want to provide a snapshot of the area in the 1840s and 1850s, thus highlighting the impending enormous changes in the make-up and lifestyle of the population of Garth Gynyd, in the development of the village of Bedlinog itself and its relationship with developments outside the valley.

The geography of the village meant that it developed as an isolated unit and even today, approaching on the road from the south, the only main road access, Bedlinog looms ahead, straggling up the mountainside in the otherwise rural north Bargoed Taff Valley: a triangle of a small built-up area surrounded by farms which lead onto open common moorland. Yet just a mile away, hidden by Merthyr mountain, lies the urban sprawl of Merthyr Tydfil and the villages of the Taff Valley.

The contrast in the early nineteenth century was even greater. Merthyr Tydfil, in 1801 the largest town in Wales, was a bustling industrial and urban centre; Garth Gynyd then was completely rural, remaining immune from the lure of the iron industry until the increased demand for coal led to the growth and industrial development of Bedlinog. Its early isolation also meant that the hamlet avoided the worst of the social problems of the neighbouring valley. Examination of the Graig Fargoed chapel registers and of consecutive decades of census material, for example, shows that the several outbreaks of cholera in Merthyr did not seem to reach Garth Gynyd.

Prior to industrialisation, therefore, Garth Gynyd was a typical upland hamlet centred on the small settlement of Cwmfelin where there was a mill and a few cottages surrounded by several farms and one or two isolated cottages on farms or on boundaries of the common.

There is early evidence of Cwmfelin Mill. Lewis Williams' will of 1672 allowed for £20 to be paid by the tenant of the Mill to each of his four daughters for the four years after his death, after which time the property would revert to the full ownership of his son, Thomas Lewis. The Mill is then mentioned in a 1688 pro-nuptual agreement as one of eighteen properties, part of the £150 marriage portion of Annie, daughter of Thomas Morgan, to William Lewis, son of Wenllian William, widow,

A water grist corn mill lately erected Melin Cwm Bargoed, with mill ponds, mill wheels, flood gates, water courses etc, formerly of Edmond David and purchased of him by Lewis William[4]

The 1801 census evokes a similar rural picture. There were twenty three occupied houses (four unoccupied) with one hundred and twenty eight people and all of the adults and older children were involved in agriculture - although it is assumed that some would have been rural craftsmen also. The 1811 census shows this more clearly when one hundred and eighteen people were counted, living at twenty four homesteads, with twenty of the families involved in agriculture and the other four in 'trade and manufacturing', probably those living in the mill and cottages at Cwmfelin which included a blacksmith's shop and an inn. In addition, from the early 18th century, Garth Gynyd Hamlet had an isolated non-conformist chapel at Graig Fargoed. The chapel on the site today dates from 1867 but bears a plaque recording that this replaced an earlier meeting house built in 1750. The cottage opposite the chapel may originally have been the minister's house although during the nineteenth century it became variously a schoolhouse (for the Sunday School) and a blacksmith's shop before being purchased by the Council, rented as a private house and demolished in the 1960s.

In 1841[5], the first date for which we have more detailed information on the lives of those who lived within Garth Gynyd hamlet, we see the people had still been little touched by the enormous changes which had been generated in the neighbouring Merthyr valley – although it is probable that farmers would have tried to increase their cash crops, dairy produce or meat, for this ready and nearby market. This was a period when rural poverty was greater than that in the towns. In the 1840s, a farm labourer earned 8s per week while those working in coalmines would receive 12-22s., hence the migration to places such as Bedlinog where jobs were to be found in the nearby emerging coal industry. There were twenty-two occupied houses in 1841 and the occupations of the heads of the four households in the little settlement around the mill at Cwmfelin were blacksmith, publican and wool weaver (a widow lived in the fourth cottage). At only two other houses in the hamlet were the heads' occupations given as other than farmer. Lewis Morgan, collier, lived with his wife at Graig Fargoed cottage but clear evidence of the trend of immigration to the coalfield area is to be found in the two households at Penmark, an isolated cottage adjoining Blainllwyna Farm where Daniel Simon, a tailor and David Richards, butcher lived in 1841. By 1851, Thomas Williams, a farm labourer from

Breconshire lived there and typically, ten years later still, his son is listed as a coal miner. Lodging at other farmhouses in 1841, however, were a tyler, a school master, a collier, a road surveyor and a navigator. 'Industrial' occupations were creeping in. Only eighteen of the one hundred and twenty eight people listed in the 1841 census had been born outside the parish of Gelligaer and of these, nine had come into the area to work as farm labourers or household servants so that certainly the families of the farms of Garth Gynyd were firmly rooted there.

Of course, there would have been many earlier changes. For example, although clearance of land for settled farming must have begun at least 2,000 years ago, land continually went into, and was taken out of, agricultural use. Dinas Noddfa, the group of platform houses on the higher, open, common land to the north east of the present-day village was deserted in the 14th century according to Lady Aileen Fox,[6] thus supporting the idea that during times of war or disease, whenever population declined, poorer agricultural areas, such as these in the higher part of Garth Gynyd, would have been deserted and the better lands occupied. Throughout history, estates have been built up and later divided while individual holdings were constantly expanded and contracted, tenanted or sold. At the time of the tithe survey in 1841, most of the South Wales major landowners owned some land in the hamlet - the Dynevor, Bute, Tredegar and Hanbury Estates,[7] for example, and we also see that the long established local family of Lewis Edwards, Bedlinog Uchaf, still owned most of the central part of the hamlet - Bedlinog Uchaf and Isaf, Llan Uchaf and Isaf as well as the mill and cottages at Cwmfelin. Professor T. V. Davies sees that in the sixteenth century, Bedlinog Isaf, Cwmfelin and Llwyn Crwn (together with Bedlinog Uchaf on occasion) were held as one holding, Tir Edmund David Jenkins[8] and this may have been the basis of the Lewis Edwards estate. Other small, local estates existed at various times and further evidence found in Professor Davies' book. He describes, for example, the thirteenth century estate of Llewelyn Fwya, whose land was known as Tir Adam ap Howel. This included Bedlinog Uchaf, Coly Isaf and Tir Jenkyn ap Rosser (part of Blaenllwyna and Nant y Ffin Farms, with Llwyn Iago, Penybanc and Cwm Llwydrew Farms in the adjoining Ysgwyddgwyn hamlet in the Rhymney Valley); the whole estate forming almost a circle of farms around the common land centred on Carn y Bugail. Professor Davies also examines Hendre Lavor, an estate covering at least Garth Gynyd and Blaenllwyna Farms. The name disappears from available documents after the sixteenth century but it had been rented to Llewelyn ap Rees of Tir Pont y Rhun (an 'uwchelwyr' family) in the Merthyr Parish in 1431 and by 1570 had been purchased by the Llancaiach Estate. A century later the Pritchards still owned Blaenllwyna which was then absorbed into the Talbot Estate some time before 1756. Garth Gynyd Farm had become the property of Morgan Thomas by 1670 and by 1756, Edmund Llewelyn owned and occupied both this farm and another smaller adjoining property.[9] Further evidence from documents relating to Garth Gynyd Farm and dating from the mid sixteenth century demonstrate how land was inherited, held in trust and how individual pieces of land have been attached to different holdings at different times. Waun Gron (field 90 on Map 2), for example, in 1842 part of Bedlinog Isaf was part of Garth Gynyd Farm in the mid sixteenth century.[10]

Very little changed physically in Garth Gynyd during the 1840s and evidence of in-migration was the most notable feature at the time of the 1851 census. Eight of the heads of the households now came from outside the parish and they and other incomers came from Breconshire, Monmouthshire, West Wales and other parts of Glamorgan, especially Merthyr Tydfil. Nevertheless, the majority of the people were still involved with farming and we must not forget that although only the occupation of 'female servant' was described in the census, female family members too would have been involved in much of the work on the farm, particularly the milking and dairy work. The other occupations mentioned mirrored those of ten years earlier - schoolmaster, mason, blacksmith, shoemaker, while one of the Edwards' sons of Bedlinog Uchaf was listed as a registrar. Heralding the future, however, two men described themselves as coalminers.

In the religious census of the same year, James Evans, the minister of the Independents at Graig Fargoed (which he said had been erected in 1715) reported that his chapel had room for 170 people and that average attendance over the year was 150 per service with twenty five children going to the Sunday School. The chapel would have attracted non-conformists from a wide area, although the hamlet itself certainly had a history of divided religious loyalties. Professor T. V. Davies, for example, writes of a dispute between Robert Davies, Rector of the parish church at Gelligaer and John Jacob of Clwydtrawscae Farm in 1677. Jacob, obviously a non-conformist, was taken to a Commission of Enquiry at the Consistory Court of Llandaff where he was accused of non-payment of tithes and it is obvious from their witness statements that the local farmers were divided between supporting non-conformism or the Church of England.[11] The other example of non-conformity in 1851 was given by William Simons, deacon at Salem (built 1830), who said that his chapel could accommodate 48 people with extra room for 100 standing and average attendance at services was 30 with 10 Sunday School children.[12]

It was during the decade of the 1860s that there were to be some physical changes - the embryonic village of Bedlinog started to emerge from the old centre at Cwmfelin. By 1861 three houses had been built at Bryn Hyfryd (now know by the English version, Mount Pleasant), occupied by a quarryman and nine colliers and their families, while another ten coal workers lived in the six houses built on land near Llwyn Crwn farmhouse. Occupiers of the farms too had begun to become involved in coal and farmers' sons or lodgers on farms accounted for another two coal tippers, two coal hauliers and six colliers. These men may have travelled just north of the hamlet to the coalmines of the Mountain Hare and Cwmbargoed district which had opened in the early nineteenth century or to South Tunnel Pit, opened 1859.[13] This would have explained the siting of another public house, the Fox and Hounds, which had been built at the north eastern edge of the village and the father and son there also described themselves as coal hauliers.

Administration was still very traditional and in 1866, at a meeting at the Harp Inn, Gelligaer, for example, it was decided to recommend to the justices that Evan Kinsey, Cwmfelin, coalminer and Thomas Davies, farmer at Nant y Ffin should be appointed as parish constables.

Examination of farm and personal bills gives a brief insight into the prices of goods and services for the people of the hamlet at this period. In 1865 both the Poor Rate (Merthyr Tydfil Union) and the Highway Rate (Gelligaer Parish) was 5d in the Pound, a 1d rise from the previous year. In the same year, Benjamin Ballard, saddler and harness maker of 21, High Street, Merthyr, charged 5s 6d for a martingale, 6d for hoops and 7s 6d for a collar and a year later, 10s for a pair of leggings. In 1869 a dog licence cost 5s and one for a horse, 10s 6d. In 1871 the Wingfield Colliery (Pencaedrain Farm, near Bargoed), sold coal at 8d per cwt while more domestic items from Price Bros of Ynysowen & Cwmfelin in 1875 were calico at 3d, 2d for lace, 1d for buttons, $1^1/_2$d for pins, 8d for ribbon and 3s 6d for a lady's hat.[14]

From the mid 1860s there had been major developments and by 1871 there were over four hundred people in seventy six houses. The hamlet retained all but one of its farmhouses; Bedlinog Isaf Farm had disappeared from the census and some of its land was built on. Houses had been built in some of the fields alongside the track leading from Cwmfelin to the original site of Bedlinog Isaf farmhouse and the rest of the land had been absorbed into Bedlinog Uchaf which was thereafter called 'Bedlinog Farm'. In addition, strips of Nant Wen, Garth Gynyd and Coly Isaf Farms were built on or being developed for the railway line as clearly shown on the 1st edition (25"–1 mile) of the Ordnance Survey map, 1875 which shows the swathe of land owned by the Great Western Railway described as 'Bargoed Taff Branch, under construction'. As well as the groups of houses at Llwyn Crwn, housing had spread northward along the river and the groups of twenty four and seven houses in Coly Row were typical of what was to be described in the 1960s as the ribbon development of the South Wales valleys. The area around the settlement of Cwmfelin too had expanded and the occupants here had a variety of jobs; there were colliers and a blacksmith, and at what was later called Black Row or Tar Pits Row, a collier, two masons, another blacksmith and an apprentice baker, while David Llewelyn, previously of Merthyr Tydfil, was publican of the Bedlinog Inn. This was - and is - the village square, having at various times, St. Catwg's church, Salem Chapel, the rugby club, the New Inn and the Bedlinog Inn, the garage, a school and a number of shops. Alun Morgan describes the physical expansion of the hamlet,

This rapid growth round the Top Pit gives the village a distinctive appearance. Commencing at the village square it winds up the hillside like a long serpent, veering in sharp bends through Lower High Street (itself on a one in three gradient) via the aptly named 'Graig' ... to Upper High Street and the barren common to the north. ... terraces branch off at unusual angles and the houses seem like limpets clinging to the rock face[15]

People had moved into the village to work in nearby pits, to sink and then work in the village pits and to work on the railway. In 1871 the majority of the households depended on coal mining with one hundred and twenty four people actively involved. Thirty three of these were under fifteen and there were also a number of women; the 45-year-old mother in law of the ostler who lived at Coly Isaf Farm, for example, described herself as a coal tipper as did six other girls aged between fourteen and twenty three living at Coly Row.

Deep Navigation, to the south of the village, opened in 1872 and part of its buildings have lately been the subject of admiration, its headgear being described as

'especially elegant...shallow, long bracing struts from the great beam engine houses, themselves braced by arched trusses extending down towards the base of the pit towers'.[16]

The Dowlais Coal Company[17] further developed coal mining, opening Bedlinog Pits Nos. 1 and 2 and South Tunnel Pit (to the north of the hamlet) in 1876. The last of the nineteenth century Bedlinog pits, Nantwen Colliery, was opened in 1883. The Great Western and Rhymney Railway Companies' line through to Cae Harris and Dowlais, opened in 1876, thus linking the village with Merthyr Tydfil in the north and Nelson to the south. The railway increased immigration and itself brought employment into the village as illustrated by the 'occupations' column of the 1881 census which includes such jobs as platelayers and engine stokers. There was now easy transport in and out of the village. Colliers were brought in from Dowlais and Cae Harris and conveyance of goods was suddenly revolutionised. Farmers, too, must have benefited from the expanding markets at Merthyr throughout the nineteenth century and also from this new means of transport for selling their goods or having items delivered to their local station. Documents exist at Clwydtrawscae Farm, for example, which record picking up items such as seed potatoes, grass seed and casks of cider from Bedlinog Station.

It is during the 1870s-1880s that we first see the name 'Bedlinog' (Bedd/bedw llwynog?) ascribed to the village. It was originally found only in the two farms, Bedlinog Uchaf and Bedlinog Isaf, and it superseded 'Cwmfelin' when the village developed on the fields of this latter farm. It was certainly in use by the 1880s when the name was used in several documents, for example, the census, the 1885 Rates Evaluation and the first edition of the O.S. map.[18] These latter two documents show that by the middle of the decade the majority of the houses of the village had been built in a pattern which is basically that of the village today. The centre was at Cwmfelin, on the junction of the Nant Llwynog with the Bargoed Taff, but focal points were also further north around the junction of the Nant Coly and the Bargoed Taff and also around Llwyn Crwn. Apart from the flat road along the valley bottom, steep roads wound up the mountainside either side of the original track leading from Cwmfelin to Bedlinog Isaf Farmhouse, and the equally steep Bedw Road and Moriah Street formed the third side of the triangle leaving only the bottom fields of Bedlinog Isaf. Much of the layout of the original fields and tracks was retained in the street and road pattern.

By 1881, therefore, Bedlinog had developed into a village where most of the households depended on the coal industry although service industries had also increased and public buildings had appeared. There were five public houses, the Fox and Hounds, the Railway, the Station, the New Inn and the Bedlinog Inn. At Cwmfelin the innkeeper at the Bedlinog Inn was John Howells while Evan Evans leased the New Inn to Edmond Davies and a house and shop at Cwmfelin to Thomas Harris who also held the lease of the quarry near Cwmfelin from the Marquis of Bute (sales to the Dowlais Iron & Coal Company). There were four grocers shops, two drapers and tailors and a boot and shoemaker in the village and that other staple of the villages of the South Wales valleys, the chapel, was also well represented. In addition to Graig Fargoed and Salem, Moriah, Gosen and Soar had been built. They must have been devout Christians. Their 'Sunday School March' around the village and confirmation by the Bishop of many children was held on the only dry day during July and August of 1888![19]

Four schools were eventually erected in the village, two juniors and two secondary while pupils went to grammar schools at Pengam, Hengoed and Bargoed. The Graig School was completed in 1889.

The village has changed very little from this time and outside the village, the hamlet's appearance has changed even less. Most of the farms still exist, although the extent of the holdings are not as they were in the 19th century; although altered and modernised, many of the farmhouses still survive. Built of local stone, pennant sandstone, which also has the property of splitting easily into roofing tiles, they stretch lengthways into the mountainside, typical long houses, the dwelling areas once connected internally to the cowsheds. All are sited close to wells or springs, most now dried up with the sinking of deep mines. Information about the houses is found in the Hearth tax of 1670.[20] A tax of 2s per hearth was placed on each household and in Garth Gynyd we find only Mary Morgan's house with three hearths and Edward Lewis and William Thomas with two-hearthed houses while the rest had only one hearth, a sign of a poor area. The traditional farm buildings would also have been built of the local stone and many of these also still survive, their function giving evidence of the type of farming practiced. Corn of some sort would have been grown as evidenced by the typical upland threshing barns which still exist. At Clwydtrawscae, for example, the barn has a storage bay separated by a bench-topped low stone wall from the threshing floor which opens onto double doors at both sides, one side having an overhang and the other a porch. Until recently, the same farm had a round pigsty and a goose pen, both typical features of upland Glamorgan.

Other important features of the man-made landscape of the area are the field boundaries, mainly dry-stone walls, also made from the local pennant sandstone with occasional boulders of erratics such as millstone grit or quartz conglomerates, the latter particularly prominent in the walls of Coly Farm at the northernmost approach to the village. The rows of trees alongside modern fences mark the sites of old hedges.

There is also documentary evidence to indicate what crops were grown in the hamlet. The tithe schedule of 1841 shows that nearly a seventh of the farmland was arable (177 acres out of 1,297), suggesting that the farmers were close to being self-sufficient. Some of the field names in the schedule give evidence of the crops grown; names such as cae bara (bread field) and cae melyn (yellow field) suggest corn of some kind, while others showed natural features such as cae'r graig and cae'r darren which are fields on the steep, rocky, fern- covered valley sides. At Garth Gynyd Farm we find cae odyn, a lime kiln, evidence that at least some of the farmers of the hamlet were using lime as fertiliser by the 1840s. Kelly's Directory of 1889 stated that the chief crops of the Gelligaer parish were oats, barley and potatoes and it is likely that the bulk of the arable area would have been devoted to these hardy crops. Farmers would therefore have harvested crops for their own and their animals' use but the emphasis then, as now, would have been on livestock farming, going hand in hand with the rights of the farms of the hamlet to graze their animals on Gelligaer and Merthyr Common.

As seen above from records of farm bills, the farmers during the pre-industrial era were not completely isolated within their community, and an important feature of their year would have been the local fairs, the most important being Marchnad y Waun, held at Twyn y Waun on the mountain to the north of the village. This was traditionally held on May 13th, Trinity Monday, and the first Mondays after September 2nd & 24th and October 10th and November 20th, although by the 19th century it had become a more frequent event. This was an opportunity to buy and sell livestock and other farm produce as well as to hire labour and have a day out. Descriptions of the fairs exist which show how they too changed with urbanisation and industrialisation. One in 1867, for example, was

...attended by considerable numbers of farmers. The show of stock, however, was not large and a very small amount of business in cattle was done. Towards the evening a great number of persons visited the fair from Dowlais, Rhymney etc. and before the night the assistance of the police was necessary to quell several fights.[21]

During the 18th century the Gryffydd Jones Circulating Schools Society had placed schoolmasters in the hamlet; in 1759/60 at Garth Gynyd Farm and 1757/58 at Clwyd y Fedw, Blaenllwyna, and a school room had also been established in the cottage opposite Graig Fargoed Chapel. An Inspector's Report on this latter school in 1847 (the comments also related to Lewis Boys School and the Rhymney Iron Co. School) said that everything at the school was generally good - although the report stated that the Welsh were generally poor and illiterate - and blamed these failings on the Welsh language and non-conformity. Welsh would have been the language of the people of Garth Gynyd at that time, and we have proof at Graig Fargoed and Salem of their main religious leanings! Even in this rural, pre-industrial community, therefore, there were continual outside influences.

Nevertheless, two decades, from the mid 1860s to the mid 1880s saw the transformation of a completely agricultural landscape into one centred around pits and a village. Unfortunately, this period of widespread employment and relative wealth was very short-lived. Bedlinog and Nant Wen Pits closed in 1924 while the twentieth century mines to the south of the village, Taff Merthyr and Trelewis Drift, are also now closed.[22]Subsequent years have seen the reclamation of these and other coal pit sites in and around the village which still retains a generally rural character, its isolation relying on its limited transport facilities as well as its geographic position.[23]

1. Unless stated, elsewhere the name refers to the hamlet as described and not to the farm of the same name.
2. Glamorgan Record Office (GRO), P/2/1.
3. For example the Aberdare, Merthyr Tydfil, Gelligaer, Rhigos and Vaynor Poor Law Union in 1896.
4. GRO, D/D Je2.
5. Population details throughout the remainder of this article have been taken from the census enumerators' books for the hamlet in 1841,1851, 1861, 1871 and 1881.
6. A. Fox, 'Dinas Noddfa, Gelligaer Common, Glamorgan. Excavations in 1936', *Archaeologica Cambrensis,* xcii (2) (1937), 247-68; A. Fox, 'Early Welsh homesteads on Gelligaer Common, Glamorgan. Excavations in 1938', *Archaeologica Cambrensis*, xciv (2) (1939), 163 – 200. Lady Aileen argued that the houses were deserted at the end of the 14th century when farmers could take advantage of a declining population both because of an outbreak of the black death and Llewelyn Bren's revolt.
7. The Hanbury lands had previously been owned by the Lewis family (Courthouse, Merthyr, Gilfach Fargoed and the Van).
8. T.V. Davies, *The Farms and Farmers of Senghenydd Lordship. Part 2. Gelligaer Parish* (Author, 1991). Much of this work is based on research of the manorial records, particularly rentals, in the Bute records at Aberystwyth.
   Could Edmund David Jenkins be of the family of Edmund Jenkins who owned (and built?) Cwmfelin Mill earlier than 1672?
9. I suggest this 'smaller property' may have been Hendre Lavor, the name of one, rather than, as previously, a composite holding. The land is probably today part

of Blaenllwyna Farm, ' Hendre', which includes the site of hut/house foundations. The name here is more likely to mean the old house or dwelling rather than the use of the word 'hendre' as a winter and permanent dwelling place, associated with 'hafod' as a summer, temporary dwelling.

10. GRO, D/DD 345
11. Professor T.V. Davies, 'A Commission of Enquiry at Gelligaer in 1677 into Tithe Payments', *Gelligaer, Vol X111* (1990), 31-41.
12. I.G. Jones and D. Williams (eds.), *The Religious Census of 1851, A Calendar of Returns relating to Wales, Vol. 1, South Wales* (Cardiff, 1976).
13. Lawrence's Coalfield Directory.
14. Author's family's bills and receipts.
15. A.Morgan, 'Bedlinog:Glimpses of a Pre-War Society', *Glamorgan Historian, Vol. XI* (Barry, 197) p.141. Alun Morgan's article discusses society, culture and politics of early twentieth century Bedlinog.
16. John Newton, *The Buildings of Wales, Glamorgan* (Cardiff, 198), p.79.
17. Part of the Dowlais Iron Company.
18. 1st edition, 1887, 6" – 1 mile
19. Gelligaer Parish Church magazine, July/August 1888.
20. E. Parkinson, *The Glamorgan Hearth Tax Assessment of 1670*, Publications of the South Wales Record Society No. 10 (Cardiff, 1994).
21. Merthyr Express, June 22, 1867.
22. Taff Merthyr was sunk in 1925 and provided employment immediately after the strike – and indeed for miners in the post war years as other pits were closing. It closed in 1993, the last in South Wales. For information and reminiscences of mining and the pre-World War 11 period, see W.H. Davies, *The Right Place the Right Time* (Llandybie,1972), W.H.Davies, *Ups and Downs* (Swansea, 1975).
23. No main road was ever built northwards, out of the village towards Merthyr Tydfil, so any 'through' traffic can only access mountain roads. The railway was closed to passengers in the 1960s but remains open as a mineral line.

Acknowledgements

I want to thank Mrs Kinsey and Mrs Bowen (nee Kinsey), Nant y Ffin Farm for their photograph of shearing day at Coly Isaf and to the late Mr. Roy Beynon of Bedlinog who gave me the photograph of the village.

Map 1 Garth Gynyd Hamlet c. 1885

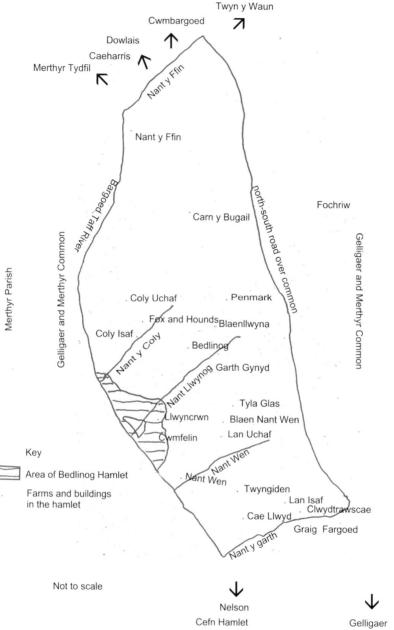

Twyn y Waun

Cwmbargoed

Dowlais

Caeharris

Merthyr Tydfil

Nant y Ffin

Nant y Ffin

Bargoed Taff River

Carn y Bugail

Fochriw

north-south road over common

Merthyr Parish

Gelligaer and Merthyr Common

Gelligaer and Merthyr Common

Ysgwyddgwyn Hamlet

Coly Uchaf

Penmark

Fox and Hounds

Blaenllwyna

Coly Isaf

Nant y Coly

Bedlinog

Nant Llwynog

Garth Gynyd

Tyla Glas

Llwyncrwn

Blaen Nant Wen

Cwmfelin

Lan Uchaf

Key

Area of Bedlinog Hamlet

Nant Wen

Farms and buildings
in the hamlet

Nant Wen

Twyngiden

Lan Isaf

Cae Llwyd

Clwydtrawscae

Graig Fargoed

Nant y garth

Not to scale

Nelson

Cefn Hamlet

Gelligaer

46

Map 2 Extract from the Gelligaer Parish Tithe Map 1841

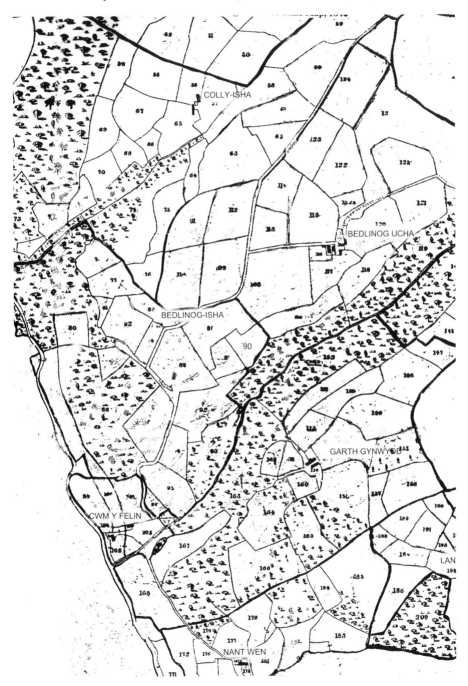

Shearing day at Coly Isaf Farm, 1922/23

From left, Tom and Annie Kinsey and their sons, Morgan, Evan, Richard, Wyndam, Elwyn and Edward, daughter Jane and granddaughter, Annie.

A WELSH INTERLUDE

~~~~~~~~~~~~~~~~~~~~~~~~

1922 - 1932

~~~~~~~~~~~~~~~

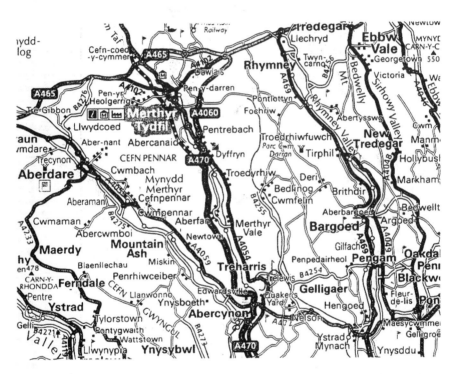

by
ALBANY HARVEY

Albert James Harvey and the Royal Army Medical Corps Concert Party 1916

A WELSH INTERLUDE, 1922-1932
by
ALBANY HARVEY

What follows is only a small part of a letter written to my three great grandsons, as a celebration of the life of my wife Eileen, their great grandmother, and of our life together. The full letter is in effect, the family history.

Dear Robert, James and Brandon,
So far you have heard about Eileen your great grandmother, who died on 19th. August 1993, when you Robert were nearly one year old. You James, and you Brandon, were not even born. She loved you very much Robert, and would have loved both James and Brandon if she had lived longer. She became very ill, too ill really to know anyone before she died, very gently and with great dignity. This was in keeping with the nature of a wonderful and very special person.

Now I will tell you about a piece of family history that covered about ten years and included my father's death in December 1925. The family and my father kept very few records and it has been a case of finding the bits and pieces and fitting them together like a jigsaw puzzle. Because the story has a beginning and an end which are dated between 1922 and 1932, I have called this particular piece an 'interlude' (a happening different in character from what comes before or after). At the end of the letter are photographs and newspaper cuttings collected at various times and in various places. I hope they give you some of the flavour of those far off times.

My father worked for the Ministry of Pensions in Newcastle and had met my mother some years before. When he was in France in the Royal Army Medical Corps during the First World War (1914-18), they used to write to each other. They had a very clever system to save space in their letters. They each had a copy of a book of poems called 'Palgrave's Golden Treasury'. Both copies are in my bookcase now. As you will see, each poem has a number and they needed only to write a number from the book in their letters, and then they would be able to read a poem saying how they felt about each other.

My father was very keen on the theatre, and while in France used to organise concerts for the troops. I have some photographs, programmes and letters from that time for you to see. He always wanted to work in the theatre or in some kind of entertainment business. When the War finally ended, they were married in South Shields on 26th. August 1919.

I, Albany Harvey, was born on 6th. January 1922, and almost at the same time my father, Albert James Harvey, got a job as manager of a cinema called THE PALACE THEATRE, in a small Welsh coal mining town called Treharris, near Merthyr Tydfil. The Welsh word 'tre' means town or homestead so the English name of the place would be Harris's town. If you look on the map you will see many other town names beginning with 'tre'. As time goes on I hope you will be able to visit many places in Wales. It is a beautiful country with everything from soft green meadows and lakes, to mountains and rocks and waterfalls, and the most friendly and kind people. Wales has a history from the earliest times when there were wars between the primitive tribes either side of what is now the border between England and Wales, through to the time when southern Wales produced more coal and steel than anywhere else in Europe.

Around 1985 there was a great battle between the miners and the government and the miners lost. The government of the day under Mrs. Thatcher set about very carefully to remove every coal mine in the country (not just in Wales) so that there is hardly a trace that there was ever a great industry which gave a nation its life blood. That is another story for you to read. As always, when you are ready for them, I have some books about Wales and its people, and about coal, and the lives of the colliers and their families, who produced it.

We moved to 23, Bargoed Terrace, Treharris. This meant that at last my father, Albert James Harvey, would be doing the kind of work he had always wanted to do. The name of the firm that gave him the job was The Albany Ward Theatre Company. To celebrate his dream coming true, and because I had just been born, I was given the only name I have - Albany. A survey of cinemas in 1914 showed that there were about 3,500 in the United Kingdom, only 210 of them being in chains of ten screens or more. The largest Cinema Circuit was that of Albany Ward with 29 screens. My brother Kenneth Robert was born in Treharris on 7th. February 1923. He lives in Hounslow in Middlesex and is great uncle to Robert, James and Brandon. Our father died on 9th. December 1925 just before I was four years old, and my brother was a year and a month and a day younger. Now was the time when our mother had to bring up two boys on a widow's pension of eighteen shillings (90p) a week for the three of us. This was why in 1932 our small family moved to Romford in Essex where lived my father's mother.

Treharris sat on the top of the Deep Navigation Colliery, which provided work for the whole community. It was created between 1873 and 1879 by Mr. F.W. Harris the Chairman of the Company. To reach the coal underground two shafts had to be dug, each of them 5·1 metres in diameter. The north shaft reached 660 metres deep and the south shaft 692 metres deep. By 1897 the Pit was owned by The Ocean Coal Company. It employed 2,500 men and boys and used 150 horses to pull the coal, in trucks or drams as they were called, along the tunnels after it had been cut. The men worked shifts to cover all day and night. To get to work they would first of all have to go down nearly 700 metres in cages to the bottom of the pit. The cages were lowered and raised up and down the shafts at high speed, on steel ropes. Having reached the bottom the men and boys would have the long walk along the tunnels cut in the coal seam, to where the last shift had finished cutting coal. When you think that the pit was sunk in 1879 and I am telling you about 1922, you can see that in 43 years the tunnels would have got longer and longer.

Perhaps you would like to think about 'what is coal ?', especially since you do not see it very often, in fact, have you seen it at all? When the world was being formed many millions of years ago there would be times when forests and all kinds of other vegetation would grow for a very long time. What we call peat was formed. New but very soft peat is still being formed especially in Ireland. Then the earth would move again or there would be some other disaster and the thick layer of vegetation would get covered over. As time went on more and more material would be washed on to, or be created from rocks and minerals so that the layer of vegetation was trapped and squeezed under the weight and heat. This was going on in what is called the Carboniferous Period about 370 million years ago. The greater the squeeze and the more any liquid and gas were pushed out, the sooner the vegetation was turned into coal and carbon, and the harder the material became. The pit in Treharris produced such material.

This coal is called anthracite, a very hard coal but clean and ideal for boilers, and in industry for making steam to drive all kinds of machines. It is not at all dirty to handle. You can imagine how, with all that weight and pressure, the coal was not only hard but squeezed very thin. This was very much the case in the older tunnels a long way away from the shaft. In some places the coal seam was only one metre thick and colliers had to cut it with a pick while lying on their sides all day long. One day perhaps, Robert, James and Brandon, your dads will take you to Blaenavon in south Wales. There the pit has been made into a museum but is run strictly to the laws and regulations for mining. This means that all visitors are kitted out with all the safety equipment and lamps before going underground with the guides to see what life was really like when working deep underground.

While we were living in Bargoed Terrace, our neighbours included George and Phyllis Williams and later their two daughters, Anne and Frances Shirley. George and Phyllis have died and Anne and Shirley now both live in West Wales. This is a lovely part of Wales near the Prescilly Hills and Pembrokeshire, and is the place from where the huge blue stones were dragged all that long way to build Stonehenge. Anne is married to Jeff Frost and they have a daughter Leigh. Shirley was married to Al Bridger until he died many years ago. Both families now live in stone houses next door to each other just over a mile from the village. Anne and Jeff still run a smallholding and sell all kinds of plants and tomatoes and leeks and other things from it.

George was a stonemason - that is, he prepared headstones and other things for graves. He had a workshop in a small corrugated iron shed built on the side of the Navigation Hotel in the town square in the middle of Treharris. The last time I was there a few years ago it was being used as a garage. I spent hours when a boy (I was aged nine plus when we left Treharris) watching George at work cutting inscriptions in marble or granite stones. The ones in marble were drilled with small holes at the bottom of each letter, then lead was beaten into the letters and the holes, so that the lead would hold in and last for years. The ones in granite were cut in a V shape and had to be cut perfectly because granite cannot be repaired easily - if at all - if a big piece is broken out. The stone was cleaned and the letters painted with a special varnish which was allowed to partly dry. With a very soft brush George would then lay a very thin layer of pure gold leaf into the letters and burnish them so that they were bright and would also last for many years. If you go into any churchyard you will see this kind of work. George tried to make his work perfect. He could not bear to make something which was only just 'good enough'. When you are older and go to work, or have a hobby making things, boys, you will find the joy of creating a beautiful object, as near perfect as possible. George did this every working day of his life. He was a wonderful man.

Sometimes I went with George to a cemetery where he had to put a new inscription on a headstone or plinth. Welsh people were very keen on burial, rather than cremation, so in those days, there were plenty of inscriptions to be done. Sometimes the stones were very heavy and it would cost a lot of money to take them to the workshop and back, or even to move them on site. Therefore I have seen George lying on his side in front of a large headstone on a plinth, with the last space for an inscription. He drew the lines with chalk, where the letters were to go and then cut them with his chisels. It was a joy to watch this superb craftsman produce lettering and decoration in the hardest material in the most unfriendly working conditions. He would start at one end, and was so skilled that by the time he reached the other end, the inscription was dead in the middle.

Other times I would deliver some coffin plates for him. A coffin plate was much loved by Welsh people. It was a steel or brass sheet in the shape of a shield and brightly chromium or nickel plated but very decorative. George would engrave by hand on the shield all the things about the dead person that the relatives wanted said. The plate would then be screwed on top of the coffin. This work came to George from the undertakers, and I often went by bus to Nelson to deliver the plates or bring them back. The ancient buses around the area were really noisy boneshakers and you could see the road through the cracks between the floorboards. I seem to remember them being called 'The Red Devil' and 'The Yellow Peril'.

George was a very gentle, kind and easy going man, and I suppose he took the place of my father. He played violin in the Tabernacle Orchestra, and at the Palace Theatre where my father Albert James Harvey was manager. Those were the days when the films in the cinema were silent. Sound on films had not been invented. An orchestra was in the 'pit' in front of, and below, the screen. Its job was to play music to match the mood of whatever film was showing on the screen. The members of the orchestra had to be very skilled and alert. They had to be sure that the music also matched the words printed on the screen to tell the story of the film. One minute they might have to play something slow and dreamy for a love scene, and the next something fast and furious for a cowboys and indians chase. Later in this 'Interlude' the programme for a concert on 22nd. February 1925 is reproduced, and in it you will see the range of music played by the Tabernacle Orchestra for the Cinema.

There were always two films in the programme, the main one and what was called a B film. Then there was a Pathe Gazette newsreel. Often there were slides which were shown on the screen to advertise a busines or some products or a message to someone in an emergency. Although I was only four when my father died, I can remember two things involving George and my father. One was that always in the passageway of 23 Bargoed Terrace were some of the large, round steel cans carrying the reels of film on their way to or from other cinemas after use. The other clear memory is of the two men sitting in the front room at the big table covered with a dark chenille cloth and with sheets of newspaper on top. They had a crystal radio set (much like the one I gave you at Christmas 2002). They had it in a big enamel bowl to make the tiny sound get louder as they tweaked the crystal tuner. Your crystal sets, boys, and theirs, are eighty years apart, but the same technology.

It happened that working part time in the theatre was an usherette named Phyllis Locke. An usherette, as today in some places, was someone who had a torch and showed people to their seats in the dark cinema. She sold ice creams in the interval and normally had a peaceful time except on Saturday mornings - more about that in a moment. George and Phyllis fell in love and married and came to live at No. 23 for a time until they moved to their own place at 15A. Later Anne and Shirley were born. Phyllis was the one who ran the house and managed the family, at a time when money was getting very tight. There were so many stonemasons that they were cutting prices to get the work, which was growing less because people could not afford expensive memorials. This was the beginning of the great disaster of the 1930's when there was hardly any work and people went hungry. If you boys would like to know more about those times, as always, I have some books.

This was a time when the pits closed and men were unemployed for a very long time. They had nothing to do and risked being caught by the police for raking over the waste tip above every colliery for a few lumps of coal to make a fire. This was when families had to apply for a small amount of money from the government to live on. It was a condition for getting this money that first they sold everything that was not essential for living. This was the time when parents quietly went without food themselves in order that their children would eat. Despite all this the Welsh way of life survived through the Depression, as it was called in the 1930's. What happened to the people made more and more of them resolve that never would their children have to go through the same kind of experience. The Welsh had always been a nation of books and learning and music, and still are. This is why there are so many doctors, lawyers and other professional people, and rugby players, all seeking to make a better life even if it means leaving their motherland.

To return to the Palace Theatre before the time we left Wales to live in Essex. Every Saturday morning was given over to children and childrens' films. Looking back now, I wonder how the staff managed to cope with us scruffy little monsters. The cinema doors were fitted with crash bars so that they could be opened from inside but not from the outside. On the inside of the doors hung heavy curtains to keep out any light. This made the means for a battle of wits between us boys and the usherettes. We would either plot out the door where they were furthest away, or start a small fight to keep their attention when the film meant the lights were low. It was then a matter of very quickly and very quietly cracking the door open, getting a few of our mates in behind the curtain, closing the door against any light and then creeping out to the nearest empty seats without paying

We must have seemed like monsters because we always carried a supply of oranges and monkey nuts with us. By the time the film was under way, pieces of peel and empty shells were available for pelting the screen when the villians appeared. It is not easy to remember all the details from seventy years ago but I seem to remember seeing a film 'Fu Manchu' the Yellow Peril and master criminal, which was a serial. This meant that each instalment ended at an exciting point so that you had to go next week to see what happened. Like the films you see today, there was no way the hero could escape certain death - but he always did. A few years later in 1939 there was another famous serial 'The Lone Ranger'. This had a masked rider, his assistant Tonto and horse named Silver. They went about the wild west doing good deeds and bringing villians to justice. Then of course, there was always Mickey Mouse in black and white only.

Adults had such first time films as 'Dracula' with Bela Lugosi and 'Frankenstein' with Boris Karloff, both in 1931, which saw the beginning of the 'talkies' when films had sound for the first time. The whole cinema industry changed and of course there was no longer any need for orchestras in the pit. Nowadays you boys get one monster film which blasts your ears, plus long adverts, which are the same as you have already seen on television and in the newspapers, plus very little choice of programmes. Then there are the 'refreshments' which can only be described as a rip-off. If you compare this with the programmes we used to have, I think we had the best bargain and the greater enjoyment.

One advantage we boys had when growing up in Wales was the lack of traffic, the streets could be our playgrounds. We played with spinning tops, five stones, tip cat (a piece of wood sharpened to a point at each end and struck with a stick to make it jump the furthest distance), a hoop - a steel ring about 85 centimetres diameter which was struck with a stick to make it roll forward. The skill was to make speed by weaving in and out of other hoops without making contact. Other games were with marbles and cigarette cards. The last named was a complicated game of stacking up and knocking down cigarette cards. Nearly all the cigarette makers put these cards in the packets to attract buyers. Many of them were real works of art and many were issued as sets to encourage smokers to keep buying to complete a set, and be given an album or other gift.

In the Square in Treharris was a shoe repairer named Ben Clee in a tiny shop. It was a meeting place for his friends who all smoked. Most days I would call there and have his permission to search through the cigarette packets on the floor for the cards. They were as good as money for swapping to make up sets. In a small way they were also a mark of being ever so slightly better off. A packet of cigarettes with a card was packed in a cardboard box and with a silver paper lining. The alternative was known as a 'Woodbine' - five cigarettes in a paper wrapper open at one end. I think there was an option when times were bad (as they were in the 1930's) to buy them one at a time. I had a valuable contact in the person of Arthur Jones, the schoolmaster's son. I could visit him now and again to play - joy upon joy - with his Meccano set. I do believe that other boys were permitted this pleasure because none of us could even think of owning such a luxury.

There are some tales about 'going up the mountain'. You will understand that in an area full of mountains, most of the time you are either walking uphill or walking downhill. Bargoed Terrace goes east and west and up and down. At a cross road by St. Mathias Church it becomes Brynteg. The road crossing runs north and south. Steeply south it ends up over the railway into Quakers Yard on its way to Cardiff. Very steeply north it 'goes up the mountain' and can eventually reach Merthyr Tydfil, but it is a long walk over the top.

We boys used to content ourselves with going up to where the rows of houses ended and wait for the coal carts to come up. Every house had a coal cellar reached by a path from the hill. The only way to deliver was by horse and cart because there were very few lorries in 1932 and they were not very powerful anyway. Imagine the scene in the half dark, especially on a cold icy morning. Two horses in tandem hauling a large cart full of coal for houses near the top (the lower ones having already taken deliveries). The road made of stone chippings, already hollow in the middle from countless hooves trying to get a grip. The horses have already come uphill from the pit and have to climb another steep slope from St. Mathias Church straight up the mountain without being able to get a run at it.

These are beautiful huge animals decorated with shining brass medals and plates on their harnesses, which glitter like gold in the light from the driver's lamp. As they take the strain of the load, even two horses in tandem find the going tough as they stamp their hooves into the roadway. As they slowly tackle the slope, the horses send up clouds of steam from their sweat, and showers of sparks from their steel shoes striking the stones. The driver shouted to the horses to encourage them, and we lads added our own shouts, especially when a horse lost its grip on the road and the driver had to juggle the brakes to get control. Then on the way back down, we witnessed the skill of the driver in using his brake to let the horses get down the slope without slipping or falling.

There was the never to be forgotten time when disaster struck while the horses were hauling telegraph poles up the mountain, I think to a farm at the top for some kind of land line. A pole broke loose and soon gathered speed heading south. Diagonally opposite the Church at the corner of Brynteg was (is) a ladies' dress shop, which received the telegraph pole through the window until it came to a stop in the back room. Fortunately, no one was injured but you can imagine how the word spread like wildfire and kept conversation going for days.

The other story concerns toilet paper. In 1931 toilet paper, as we know it today, cost too much. The toilet was usually down (or up) stone steps in a brick shed, half of which also served as the coal cellar. The toilet was a wooden seat the width of the compartment, with a hole in the middle leading into the china bowl beneath. The seat might or might not be fitted with a hinged lid. The chain to flush the toilet was close by, along with a hook. The routine was to tear up the newspapers to a convenient size and spear them onto the hook by one corner. The odd thing is that I can never remember the paper giving up black ink like today's papers do. Sears Roebuck mail order catalogues were favourite in America if you had friends or relatives there who could arrange a supply. The pages were soft and absorbent. Also in use was a real prize if you were in the right place at the right time. Large Jaffa oranges were packed in boxes, and each orange was individually wrapped in tissue paper. These tissues were just the right size and were highly prized. Rumour had it, but I cannot say if it was true, that these 'toilet papers' were reserved for visitors.

I thought I had reached the end of the story of this particular interlude when, by great good fortune, I did a last random trawl through the internet using the key words 'Albany' and 'Ward'. I found a commercial directory containing details of a firm in Kettering with a contact named Mr. R. Albany-Ward (Richard). This led me to his father Mr. A. Albany-Ward (Tony), whose father was the man who gave my father that job of manager of the Palace Theatre in Treharris. We have made contact with each other. More than that, I found an internet site run by a lady named Birdie Johnson in Minehead in Somerset. She produces what is called 'Oral History', which is made up of recordings of very old citizens talking about their lives and their adventures. This means that the past can be captured before it is too late and while the storyteller is still able to remember details and to communicate them.

In this case there is a recording of Mr. Ken Baker who recently died at I think age 95, and I have a copy of the disk. He tells of his experience as chauffeur to Mr. Albany Ward in Taunton and about Mrs. Albany Ward and about their son Tony, and his own son Richard (with both of whom I have made contact). This means that after 81 years we have made a clear cut link to the past --

My father Albert James Harvey ---- Albany-Ward
Anthony (Tony) Albany-Ward ---- Albany Harvey (me)
(we were born about the same time)
Richard Albany-Ward
and other Albany-Ward family members.

I do hope you find this, and the other pieces of our family history, interesting and that you are tempted to read some more about the way people lived in the past - and made the present. Remember that as you live your lives, you are making the new history of the family at this very moment. Why not think about recording it by keeping interesting photographs and articles and your own stories as well as the tapes and discs that modern technology makes possible for us all to have.

Because many people have done this, there is a huge amount of information about everything for you to get at (should the word be 'access'?). The internet carries a great deal of information and points the way to more, but the genuine article is much more attractive. Local libraries and Public Records Offices are the places to go for original documents. You will find that when you become really interested in a subject and want to know more, you will end up in one of these places. There is nothing quite like calling for an ancient document and finding that it may not have been opened for a hundred years. Without thinking, you will automatically treat it very gently - probably with gloves - carefully turning the pages and imagining what the person looked like who wrote the words so long ago. Your mind then wanders to think about what his or her life and family were like, and before you know it you are hooked and following new clues about the past, as well as making your own new history about the present. Happy hunting boys.

This item was written in July 2003 by --
Albany Harvey, 18, Southchurch Boulevard, Southend on Sea, SS2 4XA,
who is very grateful :
to Carolyn Jacob, Merthyr Central Library, for her help and advice,
to Edwina M. Turner and Sally Uphill at the Western Mail and Echo who so kindly
replied to my appeals for press cuttings and photographs,
to Lynne Carlick at Treharris Library who did the same,
and to all those who allowed themselves to be mentioned in this recalling of an episode
over eighty years ago.

NOTE

Notes from Mr. Dyson, manager of 150 seat cinema THE REX in Wareham, Dorset, referring to Albany Ward. The author of the note is not known.

Dear Sir, I note your request for information on local cinemas in the *Free Portland News* and append the following which may be of some assistance.

I joined Albany Ward Theatres as rewind boy at the Palace Theatre, Easton, in 1926, or 1927. At that time Albany Ward, whom I never met, ran a chain of small cinemas in the West Country including the Channel Islands. I understood that he had originally run a travelling Theatre 'Barnstormers' in the area, and certainly many of his staff were ex-actors. At that time the circuit manager was J.D. Saunders, who had a couple of circuit inspectors to assist, one of whom was Charles (?) Duncan, a large man who used to play the 'Heavy' in the touring company, the circuit engineer was named Peerless and was assisted by a man called Best.

Albany was always spoken of with awe by those who knew him and was reputed to have a fabulous home in the West Country, decorated in cinema style, he was certainly an astute business man and ran his own printing company. This was the Salisbury Press at Salisbury, at which all the playbills for his theatres were printed, and I believe also that Albany Ward had a Decorating Company to refurbish his theatres.

Some time after I joined the chain was taken over by Provincial Cinemagraph Theatres (PCT) and later became part of the Gaumont British Circuit. I was with them in all about seven years and then went on to work for the Bravery Group who had a small chain in the Poole and Bournemouth area.

When I started, the Palace at Easton was managed by a Mr. Best who left soon after to become circuit engineer assistant, the chief operator was George Bigwood who became manager on Best leaving, he continued in the managerial role and I met him some years later when he was in charge of a new place, I believe in Bath.

The Easton Palace was in Park Road at the junction with Easton Square and was an old Methodist Church, the new Church being at the other end of the Square where it still is; the old Palace after it closed became a Youth Club and stood until some five years ago when it was pulled down and became two houses. The staff comprised manager, doorman, cashier and two or three usherettes. And a man who used to sit in the front rows 'to keep the yobs quiet', a pianist, and of course the operator and rewind boy (who also did the bill-posting).

Power was supplied by a single cylinder engine running on town gas, belt driving a D.C. dynamo, there was also a petrol driven back up plant (very shaky). Performances were evening only with a matinee on Saturdays, never on a Sunday. An innovation towards the latter part of my stay there was the providing of a gramophone and amplifier by Messrs. Marshall to play records before the performance started, which was accompanied by a flashing logo mounted above the proscenium. I am quite unable to say when it closed down.

The Palace at Victoria Square in Portland was located in the lower hall of the Masonic Hall which is still used for functions, it also had its own power supply mounted under the stage with the dynamo mounted on a raised pedestal, to clear the flooding to which the area is subject and providing an additional spice to the shows in heavy weather. The manager was Alfred Case, a real trouper who had been both villian and comic relief as necessary in the 'Barnstorming' days. His name always appeared on the playbills as manager of both Easton and Portland Theatres so I take it the Easton manager was only considered to be an assistant. The operator was I think called Jack Hide or Hynd and would slip off the engine belt when flooding threatened, the engine itself appearing to come to no harm under water. I can remember peering down through a trapdoor in the stage at the dynamo on its pedestal, sticking out of the water like an island.

Films for both these cinemas were transported by rail, but later Film Transport Services started up which meant they were changed over during the night or early morning instead of someone (the rewind boy) having to get up to catch the early train.

Mr Brian Young, Lenzie, Glasgow is thanked for his assistance.

lring raised to the aldermanic bench. Notice in this case must be given him (the Town Clerk) by two burgesses residing in the ward, and an election must take place within fourteen days.

PROPOSED MOTOR 'BUSES.—The Town Clerk also reported that the question of providing a service of light motor 'buses in the borough would be considered by the joint committee at an early date, and he hoped a report would be submitted to them at the next meeting of the Council.

ENTERTAINMENT OF AMERICAN SAILORS.—The Town Clerk reported that the entertainment of 400 of the sailors of the American Fleet and 200 of the English bluejackets took place at the Pavilion on Friday, Nov. 25th, and he ventured to say that it gave the greatest satisfaction to the men. That day another Division of the American Fleet was to arrive, and it would be for the Council to consider and decide what steps should be taken for their entertainment during their stay here. The Mayor and Mayoress entertained the officers to a dance at the Royal Hotel, which was greatly enjoyed by them, Admiral Sir William May and Lady May, Admiral Sturdee and Mrs. Sturdee and several distinguished military officers being also present. The Town Clerk added that the steamers which brought the American sailors to the Pavilion for the municipal entertainment were furnished by Messrs. Cosens and Co., who declined to receive any remuneration. He was sure the Council would desire to express their appreciation of the firm's kindness. (Applause.)

The Council went into committee at 1.30.

WEYMOUTH AMUSEMENTS.
PAVILION THEATRE.
SACRED CONCERT.

Fate—or rather a dismal succession of wet Sundays—seems bent on denying to the sacred concerts in the Pavilion Theatre that full measure of success which the quality of these delightful entertainments to justly entitle them to. There was no exception to what is now regarded as a general rule on Sunday, and a day of almost continuous rain put a decided damper upon the sacred concert in the evening, and the attendance was depressingly small. Mr. Phillpott, a promising Weymouth tenor, had been engaged for the evening, and he sang faultlessly in "When I survey" (Lawrence Hope) and "The Lord is my Shepherd" (Joseph Adams). The following was the full instrumental programme :—

. March, "Cadiz" (Valverde); Illustration, "Waldesflustern" (Twitterings in the Woods) (Czibulka); reverie, "Douce Visions" (Aletter); violin solo, "Kleine Liebling," Mr. E. Mawer; overture, "Raymond" (Thomas); 'cello solo, Mr. Lionel Taylor; strings, "Andante Cantabile" (Tschaikowsky); intermezzo, "Paquita" (Darewski); finale, "Songs without Words" (Lieder ohne Worte) (Mendelssohn).

Latest evidence of Mr. Ward's enterprise is greatly appreciated.

BELLE VUE PICTURE PALACE.

The Belle Vue Picture Palace, Mr. Albany Ward's latest venture, was opened on Monday night, when a programme of surpassing excellence was presented to an audience, delighted both with the entertainment itself and the new picture palace in which it was given. At the Belle Vue Picture Palace Mr. Ward has laid himself out to cater for his patrons in his usual liberal and up-to-date style, and he has also provided for their comfort in a manner which will meet with the highest commendation. The new place of entertainment is splendidly furnished, the appointments being arranged in the greatest taste. The draperies are daintily hung and give a delightful suggestion of warmth to the interior of the building. The floor is a sloping one, a clear and unobstructed view of the screen thus being provided for everyone. An innovation that will probably be appreciated is that the more expensive seats are at the back of the hall, the cheaper ones being immediately beneath the screen. The seating accommodation is excellent and the arrangements altogether are worthy of the highest praise. The hall is run on the two-houses-a-night system, the first entertainment commencing at seven o'clock and the second at nine o'clock. The programme which Mr. Ward submitted on Monday night was quite up to the standard which he has set up at his other place of amusement, the Jubilee Hall, and that it was thoroughly appreciated by the audience was testified by their frequent outbursts of applause. The programme was—as it will always be—entirely pictorial, the depictions being of the usual varied and representative character. Comic, dramatic, and pictures of general interest succeeded one another on the tastefully got-up screen, from which the eyes of the audience were never allowed to roam. "The Shepherd's Kiss" was a beautifully coloured picture of dramatic qualities and of intense interest. To those of a sensational turn, "The Forest Rangers" made a very strong appeal, for it is full of incident of the most exciting nature. A picture full of educational interest was that showing the means of transit employed by the Chinese, the beautiful scenery also shown in the picture being greatly appreciated. There are many other instructive and dramatic films, all of the highest interest, and the comic subjects are irresistible, especially funny being "Tontolini steals a Bicycle," "The Family Feud," and "Sleepy Sam." The cinephone—animated pictures and singing combined—also occupies a prominent place on the programme. So long as Mr. Ward provides programmes of this week's excellence there can be no doubt that the Belle

The kind of entertainment provided by the very energetic Mr Albany Ward
This account is from "The Southern Times" in Weymouth on December 10th. 1910

A typical "Magic Lantern" of Albany Ward's pre film days

WITH THE BRITISH EXPEDITIONARY FORCE

Y.M.C.A.   Y.M.C.A.

Remount Depôt
Peuplingues
14/10/15

Address reply to

Y.M.C.A.
C/o A.P.O 4.
B.E.F.

Oct 19th 1915

Dear Mr Harvey

Just a line to express my appreciation of the Concert Party which visited our hut at Peuplingues on the 14th inst. I spoke to many of the men afterwards & they all said they had had a good time & hoped you would come again.

I can assure you that the care taken in choosing the costumes & in introducing the original sketches into some of the items were not lost sight of by the audience, & the performance appealed to the men because it was something new.

Wishing you every success in your future performances

I remain,
Sincerely yours,
Frank E. Thomas.

Lcp. A.T. Harvey.
R.A.M.C.
A.D.M.S. Office

Leader.
Y.M.C.A. Hut.
Peuplingues.

63

Albert James Harvey 1922

Town Hall,
Merthyr Tydfil.

5th. February 1923.

Dear Mr Harvey,

GELLIFAELOG RELIEF FUND.

In acknowledgement of your cheque for £30. 6. 11d, I have pleasure in forwarding receipt herewith, also letter for transmission to Mr Albany Ward.

I congratulate you on the excellent manner in which you organised the Concert which resulted in such a substantial sum being realised for the Fund.

Please convey to all the members of your staff and all who assisted my sincere thanks for their services.

I may add that the Mayoress and myself thoroughly enjoyed the performance.

Tanking you again for your kind assistance.

With kindest regards,

Yours faithfully,

Mayor.

Albert J. Harvey, Esq.,
      The Palace,
            TREHARRIS.

65

We, the undersigned, being members of a Committee elected from the Staff of the Palace Theatre, Treharris, beg to bring to your notice, the case of Albert E. Watkins, of 11 Webster Street, Treharris, Town Crier.

As is generally known, Watkins is blind, having been so from the age of six years. Some five years ago he was examined and told there was no hope of his ever regaining sight. Since attaining the age of 28 years, however, he has felt pain in his eyes and has been able to distinguish between light and dark. Thinking that this might be due to functional changes, which as is known take place every seven years, we have had him examined and find that there is a hope of his regaining, by proper treatment and possibly an operation, the sight of his left eye.

We have, therefore, formed a Committee with a view to running a Concert, the whole of the proceeds to be devoted to taking Watkins to a Harley Street, London, Eye Specialist, for thorough examination and possibly the operation mentioned. We have arranged for examination by Doctor Leslie Johnston Paten who is one of the finest Eye Specialists in the Country. Watkins has placed himself unreservedly in our hands and is perfectly willing to undergo the operation, if necessary. Although in the past a Concert was held to start Watkins in business—which failed—we are setting out with a greater object in view. We think that if this object, of getting Watkins' sight back succeeds everyone connected with the means of raising the funds—from patrons, ticket sellers, artistes, etc., may well be proud of the achievement. We think it advisable to state that all monies will be handled only by the Committee and a proper balance sheet will be published.

We have prepared an excellent programme as follows :

Instrumental : The Tabernacle Orchestra under the Conductorship and by kind permission of Mr. Oliver Eynon.

Vocal · The Welsh Gleemen (Troedyrhiw) under the Conductorship and by kind permission of Mr. Herbert Llewelyn.

Pictorial : The Enchanted Cottage—featuring Richard Barthelmess and May McCoy—kindly loaned free of all charge by Messrs. The Associated First National Pictures Ltd., London.

The Theatre has been kindly loaned free of all cost by the Managing Director of the Lessees. The Staff including an Augmented Orchestra for the picture are giving their services gratis.

We have fixed the prices as low as is possible to allow us the amount of money necessary for the project. The Balcony will be 1/6 with no extra charge for booking. The Back Stalls 1/- and the Front Stalls 8d. Exemption from Tax has been granted by the Commissioners of Customs and Excise.

The cause without a doubt a good one, and we ask you to take a ticket from our sellers when they visit your residence. In return we promise you a first class entertainment—and the gratifying knowledge that you, for one, have done your little best in helping to give to one poor soul, life's greatest gift—sight.

George Barnes, Chairman, 14 Pritchard Street.

Edward Rosser, 16 Railway Terrace.

George S. Treziss, 4 The Park.

Haydn Davies, Treasurer, Brynteg Terrace.

Albert J. Harvey, Secretary, 23 Bargoed Terrace.

PALACE THEATRE,

TREHARRIS.

PROGRAMME

of GRAND

CONCERT

to be held on

Sunday, February 22nd, 1925.

Proceeds in aid of Fund instituted with a view to taking
Mr. A. E. Watkins to a Harley Street, London, Eye
Specialist, for examination and possibly an operation,
it having been ascertained that there is a possibility of
his regaining the sight of one eye.

Chairman - - - Captain D. G. Richards, M.C.

The Committee wish to tender their sincere thanks to the
following :— Managing Director of the Lessees of the Palace
Theatre for the use of the Theatre.

Messrs. Associated First National Pictures, Ltd., for the loan
of the film " The Enchanted Cottage."

T. Grayson, Esqr., St. Helens, Lancs., for Cheque for
Expenses.

The Tabernacle Orchestra for services.

The Welsh Gleemen for services.

Mr. W. G. Evans, The Graig, for conveyance of The Welsh
Gleemen.

All ticket sellers and helpers.

The Orchestra and Staff of the Palace Theatre for services.

PROGRAMME - - - - - - PRICE 2d.

G. Barnes, *Chairman.*   Haydn Davies, *Treasurer.*

Albert J. Harvey, *Secretary.*

67

PROGRAMME.

PART 1. INSTRUMENTAL.

8 p.m. THE TABERNACLE ORCHESTRA (Treharris) under the Conductorship and by kind permission of Mr. Oliver Eynon.

1. Overture	...	...	"Pique Dame"	...	...	*Suppe*
2. Symphony	...	1st Movement of "B Minor" Symphony				*Schubert.*
3. —	—	...	"Praeludium"	...	...	*Jarnefelt.*

8.30 p.m. Address by the Chairman, Captain D. G. Richards, M.C.

PART 2. VOCAL.

8.35 p.m. The Welsh Gleemen (Troedyrhiw) under the Conductorship and by kind permission of Mr. Herbert Llewelyn.

As many of the following items will be rendered, as time permits:

1. Chorus	...	...	"The Hallelujah"	...	...	*Handel.*
			THE GLEEMEN.			
2. Duet	...	...	"The Battle Eve"	...	...	*Bonheur.*
			Messrs. EDWARDS and HORTON.			
3. Solo	...	...	"It is enough"	...	...	*Mendelssohn.*
			Mr. BEN LEWIS.			
4. Part Songs	(a)	"Hen Wr Mwyn"	...	...	*arr. Llewelyn.*
	(b)	"Cyfri'r Geifr"	...			
			THE GLEEMEN.			
5. Solo	...	Selected	...	...	...	
			Miss GWLADYS MORGAN.			
6. Duet	...	...	Melodrama	...	...	*Idlam.*
			Messrs. DAVIES and GRIFFITHS.			
7. Chorus	...	...	"The Tyrol"	...	...	*J. Thomas.*
			THE GLEEMEN.			
8. Solo	...	...	"Yr Hen Gerddor"	...	...	*Evans.*
			Mr. GWYNLAIS JONES.			
9. Solo	...	...	"Largo al Factotum"	...	...	*Rossini.*
			Mr. STEPHEN GRIFFITHS.			
10. Chorus	...	...	"Miserere Scene"	...	...	*Verdi.*
			THE GLEEMEN. Duet Miss MORGAN and Mr. G. EDWARDS.			
11. Duet	...	"Trot Here and There" (from *Veronique*)				
			Miss MORGAN and Mr. LEWIS.			
12. Solo	...	...	"Monarch of the Storm"	...	...	*Mullin.*
			Mr. S. HORTON.			
13. Cycle of Welsh Hymn Tunes				...	...	*arr. Llewelyn.*
			THE GLEEMEN.			

PART 3. PICTORIAL.

9.10 p.m. "THE ENCHANTED COTTAGE."
Kindly loaned by Messrs. Associated First National Pictures, Ltd. London.

CAST OF CHARACTERS:

Oliver Bashforth, late Lieut. 8th Batt. Royal Fusiliers	...	...	...	Richard Bartlelmess
Mrs. Smallwood, his Mother	...	...	Ida Waterman.
Rupert Smallwood, his Step-father	...	Alfred Hickman.
Ethel Bashforth, his Sister	...	...	Florence Short.
Beatrice Vaughn, his boyhood Sweetheart	...	Marian Coakley.
Major Murray Hillgrove, D.S.O., M.C.	...	Holmes E. Herbert.
Laura Pennington	...	...	...	May McAvoy.
Mrs. Minnett	...	...	...	Ethel Wright.

Directed by John S. Robertson from the Stage Success by Sir Arthur Wing Pinero.

The drama of a disabled war cripple and a plain woman whose love transfigures them in their own eyes into people of infinite beauty.

PROGRAMME OF MUSIC to be played by the Palace Orchestra during the projection of the Film. Conductor Mr. Geo. Barnes

Waltz	...	...	"The Enchanted Cottage"	...	*Rogers, Campbell and Connelly.*
Lyric Suite	...	...	"Eugen d'Albert"	...	*Guiseppe Becce.*
Andante	...	...	"Russian Cradle Song"	...	*L. Kiein.*
Intermezzo	...	...	"Pizzicato"	...	*Joseph Neary.*
Symphonique	...	...	"2 e Croquis"	...	*Jean de Smetsky.*
Suite	...	...	"La Source"	...	*Leo Delibes.*
Chanson Napolitaine	...	"Plus Belle que Jamais"	...	*G. Bonincontra.*
Minuet	...	...	"Minuet en" Marquise"	...	*D. de Severac.*
Minuet from Ballet	...	"Les Millions d'Arlequin"	...	*Richard Drigo.*
Moreau de Concert	...	"A Love Song"	...	*Haydn Wood.*
Czardas	...	...	"Cyra"	...	...	
Mazurka	...	...	"Sussex Ervarten"	...	*Fr. Michael.*
			"Chant sans Paroles"	...	*P. Tschaikowsky.*
Song	...	...	"Why are the roses so pale"	...	*P. Tschaikowsky.*
Valse Boston	...	"Adoration"	...	*A. H. Jaughert.*
			Songs without words, Op. 19	...	*F. Mendelssohn.*
			No. 1.	...	...	*Barthelmy.*
Intermezzo	...	...	"Home"	...	*H. Sullivan Brooke*
Melody	...	...	"Melodie"	...	*Moczkowski.*
Symphony	...	...	"Andante Cantabile"	...	*L. V. Beethoven.*
Overture	...	...	"Adelaide"	...	*L. V. Beethoven.*
Intermezzo	...	...	"Flirtation"	...	*Mar Rau.*
Waltz	...	...	"The Enchanted Cottage"	...	*Rogers, Campbell and Connelly.*

GOD SAVE THE KING.

Some of the things on offer in 1926

THE PALACE, TREHARRIS.

WEEK COMMENCING JUNE 28th, 1926.

MONDAY, TUESDAY & WEDNESDAY:

SYD CHAPLIN in

The Man on the Box

The screen's cleverest female impersonator in a fast, furious, femdashing farce.

SECRET SERVICE SANDERS—Episode 11.

FELIX IN BLUNDERLAND.

THURSDAY, FRIDAY & SATURDAY:

SALLY O'NEIL and WILLIAM HAINES in

MIKE

A Railroad Romance of Elsmont and Thrills.

WILD WEST—Episode 4.

MR. OLD KENTUCKY HOME—Song Cartoon.

MONDAY to FRIDAY at 7.30.
SATURDAY 2.30, 6.30 and 8.45.
Seats may be Reserved. Phone 20.

PALACE, TREHARRIS.

WEEK COMMENCING DECEMBER 6th, 1926—MONDAY, TUESDAY, WEDNESDAY.

RICHARD BARTHELMESS with DOROTHY MACKAILL in

SHORE LEAVE

Founded on the Play by Hubert Osborne.

THE POWER GOD—Episode 8.   CRADLE ROBBERS—A Comedy by "Our Gang."

THURSDAY, FRIDAY, AND SATURDAY.

MARY PICKFORD in "HUMAN SPARROWS"

A MIGHTY ACHIEVEMENT.
A WONDERFUL PICTURE.
SEE IT! YOU'LL LOVE IT!

THE GREEN ARCHER—Episode 8.   SONG CARTUNE—"TIPPERARY."

Monday to Friday Nightly at 7.30. Saturday at 2.30, 6.30 and 8.45. Wednesday morning at 10.15.   Seats may be Reserved. Phone 20.

THE PALACE, TREHARRIS.

WEEK COMMENCING JANUARY 25th, 1926.

MONDAY, TUESDAY & WEDNESDAY at 7.30
MATINEE WEDNESDAY at 10.15 a.m.

LON CHANEY, MAE BUSCH & VICTOR McLAGLEN in

The Unholy Three

An unusual romance of the Underworld.

SERIAL—BATTLING BREWSTER—Episode 14.

Comedy—FELIX BUTTS INTO BUSINESS.

WEDNESDAY.

GRAND MUSICAL NOVELTY NIGHT

Vaudeville Interlude by MRS. REES, the Popular Comedian.

THURSDAY AND FRIDAY at 7.30.
SATURDAY at 2.30, 6.30 and 8.45.

EVERYBODY'S FAVOURITE-TOM MIX, with
BLACK BESS, in

DICK TURPIN

A thrilling tale of love and adventure.

SERIAL—SUNKEN SILVER—Episode 3.

Monday Next—THE ADVENTUROUS SEX.
Thursday Next—THIEVES OF PARADISE.

TROEDYRHIW.

CHURCHES UNITE.—At St. John's Hall, on Tuesday evening representatives of the Troedyrhiw churches decided to form a united front with the view of deepening the spiritual life of the community. The Rev. J. Williams, (J.D.) presided, and the Rev. W. Price, M.A., pastor of Mount Zion Church, was appointed secretary.

CHURCH MEETING.—At Mount Zion on Monday evening the annual church meeting was held. Mr. George E. Chambers (the recently-appointed secretary) presented his [report] …

THE PALACE, TREHARRIS.

There is no lack of thrills and entertainment in Tod Browning's crook drama, "The Unholy Three," a Metro-Goldwyn-Mayer production, showing at the Palace Theatre next week. Indeed, it may be said that Browning has made more than a melodrama that will go over anywhere with a bang because it contains real heart and underworld interest. Its has much of a melodrama that will go anywhere with a bang, plenty of comedy, and not the least a career of robbery and murder. Grand musical novelty night on Wednesday, including vaudeville interlude by Mrs Rees, the popular comedian.

On Thursday "Dick Turpin's Ride to York" will be shown …

Typical Winding Gear to lower & raise the cages in the pit.

George William's original Workshop attached to the Navigation Hotel

The "Palace" in 1931 (note "Uncle Tom's Cabin")

The favourite resting place in 1936

71

Village's chance for say on institute plan

−7 FEB 1996

TREHARRIS MINERS'

By Jackie Bow

A VALLEYS community is to be given a bigger chance of having its say on plans to re-open an old miners' institute and cinema.

Proposals have been put forward to bring the building in The Square, Treharris, back into use for the former mining community.

The group behind the idea hopes to encourage input from the villagers by opening a project office in the old Barclays Bank premises by Easter.

The bank has offered furniture and carpets.

The bid to find a use for the building is being led by the Treharris Regeneration Association, a group of 12 committed locals.

"We want to know what the people in the community want done with the building," said association chairwoman Coun Glenys Evans.

"With a project office they can drop in and have a chat over a cup of tea.

"We will have a higher profile — we won't be 'those people' — and people can see or find out what is being done.

"As progress is made we will have a feasibility study."

Since it closed as a miners' institute and library, the building has been used as a cinema, a bingo hall and as an indoor market for just one week.

Ideas for future use have included refurbishing the cinema, theatre and exhibition facilities and opening an advice centre."

The project group is applying for European funds through RECHAR — which specifically helps former coalfield communities — and the national lottery's Millennium Fund.

"The building is privately owned and we want to try to buy it and refurbish it for the community," said Mrs Evans.

"It's in a terrible mess, it has been set on fire and a lot of mischief has been done but we are determined not to lose it."

72

Terminal illness in 1993

Death in the same spot ten years later

At the bottom of the unsheltered, unlit, cold steps.

74

Yours truly second from left – school playground 1932

75

George Williams and me sheltering from the rain in someone's chapel

76

THE TROEDYRHIW TOWN SILVER BAND
by
T.F. HOLLEY

INTRODUCTION

In the period 1944-47 I was a member of the 14th. Dublin Company, the Boys Brigade and played in that Company's Silver Band. I played various instruments including tenor and bass trombone and have happy memories of marching across Dublin, led by lanky Lieutenant Hector Mewes, from St. George's Parochial Hall on the north side of the river Liffey, past Lord Longford's Gate Theatre and Bethel Solomons' Rotunda Maternity Hospital, down O'Connell Street past Nelson's Pillar, over the Liffey bridge, past Trinity College, the band striking up 'Colonel Bogey', 'Blaze Away' and other lively marching tunes. And so to church parade at St. Patrick's Cathedral. Happy days! My interest in Brass Bands is therefore deeply ingrained and long sustained.

Much has been written about the history of Mr. Crawshay's Merthyr Brass Band and many of the instruments have been beautifully preserved and exhibited at Cyfarthfa Castle Museum and Art Gallery. This Band had the financial backing of a prosperous Iron Master, so money was not a concern.

It seemed worthwhile to investigate the comings and goings of one of the many local small Brass Bands, which did not have the constant backing of a rich patron. The Troedyrhiw Town Silver Band was chosen for study. The designation 'Silver' refers to the fact that the brass instruments had been silver coated, for whatever reason.

I located an evocative history of the Troedyrhiw Town Silver Band, for the period 1920-31, written by its famous long-serving conductor, Mr. Joseph Williams. This appeared in the *Merthyr Express*, in four parts, in the period 1931-32. This account recorded an extremely interesting piece of social history and documented the survival struggles and many successes of Troedyrhiw Town Silver Band, in an era of extreme economic difficulty. Mr. Joseph Williams' Band History is reproduced here, in full.

As a result of further research in the files of the *Merthyr Express*, present author T.F. Holley located accounts of Troedyrhiw Band activities for 1925, 1933, 1936, 1937 and 1939.

By good fortune, some excellent photos of Band members, taken in 1952, were provided by friend Mrs. June Loveday (born Bulford). Mrs. Loveday was the only female member of this Band and played the cornet. The talented Mr. Joseph Williams wrote cornet solos especially for Mrs. Loveday. Her father, brother and husband Tom were Troedyrhiw Band members. Mrs. Loveday also loaned other memorabilia, including 1952 membership cards for many of the Troedyrhiw Band members and items of correspondence regarding transfers of members from other Brass Bands including Dowlais Silver Band.

Transfer of bandsmen from one Band to another was done through a National Registry, based at 15, West Street, London, W.C. 2 and operated by the *Daily Herald*. A transfer could not take place until the National Registry received: a letter from the bandsman's previous Band agreeing to the transfer; his Registration Card for endorsement; and a letter from the bandsman saying he wished to transfer. Quite a bureaucracy!

In July 1937 Joseph Williams was still the Band conductor, with Mr. A.E. Jeffries as organising secretary. By September 1937 a new conductor was in place, Emlyn Francis, a member of the B.B.C. Welsh Orchestra. But Joseph Williams appeared with Band members in photos taken in 1952.

Left, back: BEN FOSTER, TEDDY CONNICK; CYRIL McCARTHY; GEORGE BURNS; RAYMOND OWENS(Treharris); OWEN DAVIES(Treharris); JOSS EVANS(Penlocks); VERNON BAILEY; JUNE BULFORD; LES ROPER; JOE WILLIAMS;   ; BILLY GALEOZZIE; BOB ROBERTS; GOMER WILLIAMS; (Birdie, head only); CLIFF FARREL; DES LONG; JACK KENYON; LONG JACK
Kneeling L to R: TOM LOVEDAY; MATT WILLIAMS; BILL FOSTER; DAI BULLFORD; TONY GALEOZZIE; CYRIL FORD; AARON BULFORD; BILLIE MORGAN
Boys VINCENT FOSTER; TERRY DEAN

JOSEPH WILLIAMS' HISTORY

FOREWORD

Thinking it a just and proper step I accept the responsibility of recording the history of the Troedyrhiw Town Silver Band, as no one else has been sufficiently interested in the matter to undertake the task. To me it is an honour to be permitted to draw up for publication the domestic affairs and public achievements of the Band.

The reader is reminded that records of all kinds are of incalculable value, hence the desire to preserve and chronicle the records of the Band; and the publication of same may have some attraction as reading matter, especially for the local public, inasmuch as such a course reveals, or at least brings to mind what glory has been won by the musicians, and the lustre it has shed on the town as a whole. Moreover, present day (1931) bandsmen may desire, after perusing the account of the conquests of their immediate predecessors, to emulate them, or such reading may so far influence them that their ambitions may be anchored to still higher ideals.

At least, it is to be hoped that the reader will pass a pleasant hour or so by the fireside in company with their fellow-townsmen and successful instrumentalists, the Troedyrhiw Town Silver Band. (Signed) Joseph Williams. 4, Bell-row, Pentrebach.

TROEDYRHIW BAND INAUGURATED

It was late in the autumn of 1920 that the Troedyrhiw Town Silver Band was inaugurated. Messrs. Henry Grant, Evan Parry and Joseph Williams, who were members of the MERTHYR VALE BAND, arranged a consultation, and the outcome of it was the Troedyrhiw Band. The initial committee was chosen at a meeting held at the Royal Oak Inn, there Messrs. J. Smith, Jerry Flynn and M. Davies were elected chairman, treasurer, and secretary respectively. On that occasion the offerings to the funds of the Band totalled fourteen pence.

A meeting was again held the following week, Mr. Richard Edwards this time taking the chair, but the official position was finally given to Mr. Edwin Tovey, who filled that post admirably for over two years. Committee men were elected, and one of their duties was to obtain financial assistance by public subscriptions, the first donations amounting to £20. This sum was immediately delivered to the custody of the trustees, Messrs. Walter Griffiths and W. Walsh.

TREHARRIS BAND LOANED INSTRUMENTS

During this period instruments were loaned by the TREHARRIS BAND, who had bought a new set. These were used for a year, when instruments were bought of Messrs. Boosey's, London. In less than twelve months the Band's debt was lightened to the extent of £120. From a loan by Mr. W. Walsh, a trombone and euphonium were purchased. Again a public appeal was made for financial aid for the Band.

NEW INSTRUMENTS PURCHASED

While Mr. E. Tovey's chairmanship was still unexpired, it was thought advisable to purchase a new set of instruments. Messrs. Hawkes & Co. were appealed to and they sent their representative down to consult and make terms with the Band Committee. The result was that the new set was bought at the cost of £550, and the old instruments were sold for £80. A bank loan was applied for, Mr. W. Burrows' recommendation producing £70, which helped to reduce the bill for musical goods by £150. It was arranged to pay the balance of the debt by quarterly instalments of £20, but it proved an unprofitable settlement at a charge of 5%. Concerts and dances were tried as money-producing devices, but on the whole these ventures were failures. Mr. Enoch Morrell, J.P., was a generous supporter and presided at most of the fund-raising events.

THE 1921 COAL STRIKE

During the 1921 coal strike the Troedyrhiw Band gave its support at carnival sports and at other functions. It went so far as Brecon and Builth in order to raise money to assist in the soup kitchens, enduring the discomfort of sleeping in hay lofts so as to cut down expenses. The soup kitchens benefited by £10.

PRESENTATION TO BANDMASTER.

A little time later an inscribed baton (value four guineas) was presented to Mr. Joseph Williams, bandmaster, as a tribute for services rendered

EVENTS

Then a band contest was held at Troedyrhiw. The test piece was played at the Girls' School and the march from the Belle Vue to the Victoria Buildings, Mr. Jones, Treherbert, adjudicating.

Concerts and dances were again resorted to, but little financial gain accrued from them.

The Band was engaged for the parade of the R.A.O.B., the Christmas Evans Lodge, Royal Oak Inn, Troedyrhiw, the proceeds being in aid of Merthyr General Hospital.

On the occasion of Mayor's Sunday at Abercannaid, Councillor L.M. Jones's Mayoral year, the Band took its share in the procedure of the day.

In the Remembrance Day anniversaries Troedyrhiw Town Silver Band did its part nobly.

When Mr. Rees Thomas won the tenor solo at the Royal National Eisteddfod, Ammanford, 1922, Troedyrhiw Band turned out to pay him tribute, at his welcome home.

In 1923 (1st. August) the Band was successful in winning a march. There were nine competitors, and the Town Band had the disadvantage of only having their new instruments but a few days previous to the contest. In the selection "Country Life", Mr. Carter, Durham, placed it fourth, and again suffered misfortune by having the music copies blown from the stands in the high wind.

The following Saturday, competing at Bargoed, second prize was recorded both for march and selection, PENALLTA BAND defeating them in the test piece.

This year (1923) an annual prize drawing was instituted, which has proved a successful undertaking.

Early in 1924 the Band competed at Ystrad Mynach, in Class C, and was successful with two firsts, the march and selection, for which cups and medals were obtained. At the same place in Class B competition, a third place was recorded.

In the end of the season competition at Whitchurch the Band secured second prize in march and test piece respectively. Two marks separated first and second places in the selection.

Mr. Edwin Tovey, a most steady worker in the interests of the Troedyrhiw Town Silver Band, received donations, £5 (late Lord Buckland) and £5 from Mr. Thomas

Matthews. These sums, and the gains from annual prize drawings, greatly helped to reduce the debt to Messrs. Hawkes and Son, London.

The Band is always conscientious in its tribute to the departed (dead) members and their relatives, whenever such occasions arise.

NEW CHAIRMAN AND SECRETARY

After a long period in office Messrs. Edwin Tovey and M. Davies (chairman and secretary respectively) desired to relinquish their posts, much to the regret of the Band. They were succeeded by Mr. W. Gibbon, chairman, and Mr. W. Jones later, while Mr. Ernest Williams became secretary for a brief term.

The Band now widened its outlook, and for the first time competed at the bandsmen's Mecca - Crystal Palace - and returned with fifth place out of thirty two contestants.

The end of the year came with annual prize drawing and audit, after which Messrs. Joseph Williams and A.W. Jones were elected chairman and secretary for the year.

A band contest was promoted at Troedyrhiw with Mr. D. Stephens as adjudicator.

In March 1924 the Band competed at Pontypridd, and carried away first prize from ten contestants. At Easter 1924 a band contest was promoted at the Girls' School, Troedyrhiw, eight bands entering; Mr. Dobbin from Pentre adjudicated. The effort was unsuccessful. That Easter Monday saw the band contesting at the Mountain Ash Eisteddfod, and from there, went to Tylorstown, and competed with seventeen bands, and coming top in test piece and in the march contest. Mr. Bufton Williams was adjudicator. The successes of the day consisted of two cups (one being a challenge cup), four medals for the basses, euphonium, and one tenor horn, and a silver cornet (valued at sixteen guineas). Mr. Emlyn Francis, 28, Brown-street, Pentrebach, a young bandsman, was acclaimed the best horn player, and was presented with the horn medal.

The next contest was at Ynyshir, which resulted in a gain of first prize in the march, and second in the test piece. Again Mr. Emlyn Francis was first in the horn player competition, Mr. Keen, director of Ynyshir Colliery, presenting him with the medal, and Troedyrhiw Town Silver Band also got the medal for the euphonium solo.

NATIONAL EISTEDDFOD AT PONTYPOOL, 1924

The Troedyrhiw Town Silver Band competed at the Royal Welsh National Eisteddfod at Pontypool, where it obtained the chief laurels, both in the march and the test piece. Lieut. J. Ord Hume, who delivered the adjudication in the crowded pavilion, said, as he had mentioned before in Wales, that a very great improvement had taken place in Class C Bands (applause). In the march past the first prize had been won very nicely and evenly. He would later give to the bands themselves the order in which they stood in the competition, but he would like to emphasise that the blowing of the brass bands was clear in every way. In fact, all the performers were worthy so far as he could hear them on the march, and the ending was very good indeed.

The winners on the march were (1) Troedyrhiw Town (J. Williams, conductor); (2) WINDSOR COLLIERY BAND (J. Radcliff, conductor).

In delivering adjudication on the playing of the selection "William Tell " Lieut. Ord Hume said that he had no hesitation at all in finding the first, second, third and even fourth in this contest. Sometimes a judge felt a little doubt, but there was none at all on this occasion. He was satisfied in every way. The first prize winner was absolutely faultless and tuneful. The second prize winner was also excellent - a good all-round performance - though there were some trifling flaws here and there. The winners were (1) Troedyrhiw Town (J. Williams, conductor); (2) CWMAMAN (R.S. Howells, conductor); (3) Windsor Colliery (J. Radcliff, conductor); (4) BLAENGWYNFI (W. Wade, conductor)

For the year Mr. David Jones, Merthyr Vale, was elected Mayor of Merthyr, and the Troedyrhiw Band was chosen to lead the procession on that Mayor's Sunday.

At the Brynmawr Band Contest, only two bands presented themselves, and it was decided to abandon the competition. The Troedyrhiw Town Silver Band assisted the promoters of this band contest to defray expenses by giving a Sunday evening entertainment, and the Band itself received hospitable treatment.

The Rhos open contest provided the Troedyrhiw Band with second prize.

(Merthyr Express. 5.12.1931.p.16.)

The Troedyrhiw Band attended the South Wales Band Festival held at Pontypridd in 1924, and secured first prize at the contest. Lieut. J. Ord Hume adjudicated. (There followed an adjudication, this has been omitted.T.F.H.)

During the summer, on the occasion of Jimmy Wilde's visit to Merthyr for exhibitions in the fistic art with other well-known exponents of the "ring", Troedyrhiw Band played before him through the town, from the Globe Hotel to the Theatre Royal.

BAND OFFICERS ELECTED, 1926

At the beginning of 1926 a general meeting of the members of Troedyrhiw Band was convened, and an election of officers and committee was made. Messrs. Joseph Williams, Victor Ford and W. Jones became chairman, treasurer and secretary respectively; the committee consisted of Messrs. W. Griffiths, Richard Evans, Aaron Bulford, J. Davies, J. Flynn and Frank Martin.

The Band went to the Pontypridd Festival, but was unsuccessful. Visits to competitions at Chepstow, Newport and Kerne Bridge produced second prizes at each of these places.

COAL TRADE DISPUTE, 1926

The coal trade dispute of 1926 again made it necessary for the Band to assist with its services in the alleviating of some of the distress that was prevalent in the borough at that time. The late Mr. A.J. Cook, in his visit to Merthyr on his tour of the country, was respectfully received, and the Band did its part heroically. Many were the make-shifts resorted to in order to raise funds to feed the famishing workless. The ladies committee organised a dance and £8 was realised. At the same place a football was raffled for, and returned by the winner, fetching later, at a sale, the sum of 16s..6d. A like procedure was adopted with a cake, this realising £1. Unfortunately the General Strike obstructed the transaction of a WHIPPET HANDICAP, making the benefit received scanty. It must be gratefully acknowledged that great assistance was rendered towards the efforts made on behalf of the kitchens by the officials of the Plymouth and Cyfarthfa Collieries; by Mr. Jones, of Troedyrhiw Farm, for granting the use of the field; and Mr. Tom Evans for haulage.

In the Co-operative Society's carnival sports the Band pulled - or rather blew - its weight.

The opening of the Tennis Courts at the Merthyr Vale Park by the then Mayor was attended by the Troedyrhiw Band, and thanks for the services were returned by the Mayor, Mr. David Davies, J.P., Pant, and Mr. Ben Bowen.

At the band contest in Cyfarthfa Park, held under the auspices of the South Wales Bands' Association, the Troedyrhiw Town Silver Band came third out of nine competitors.

At this time, by the death of Mr. J. Brinkworth, a most worthy person and a good supporter of the Band was lost. To him was paid the last tribute, and condolence was expressed and forwarded to his sorrowing relatives.

MONEY TROUBLES 1926

In this year of stress and trial money was scarce and Messrs. Hawkes and Son, London, clamoured for payment of their account for instruments supplied to the Troedyrhiw Band. The committee met to consider the matter and owing to the greatness of the pressure for the settlement of the quarterly instalment, the sum of £20 was collected (by loan). The contributors of this money were Messrs. Wm. Griffiths, Jerry Flynn, Wm. Jones, Joseph Williams, Louis Rossi and Richard Ellis. Later a concert was held at the Cinema, the takings enabling the Band to repay the above loan. The annual prize drawing for that year totalled £20 of profit, the Band acknowledging its indebtedness to the tradespeople, and to Mrs. Edwards, Cottrell-street, and Mrs. Williams, The Grove, for their services to the cause at Aberfan and Merthyr Vale.

On the success of Mr. J. Maldwyn Thomas, Aberfan, at the Royal National Eisteddfod of Swansea, the Band again proclaimed its appreciation in the usual manner.

Mayor's Day of the late Mr. Llewelyn M. Francis, Penydarren, was again an active one for the Band.

MONEY TROUBLES 1927

The year 1927 opened dismally for the prospects of the Band. Proceedings were threatened by Messrs. Hawkes and Son to recover debt incurred to them for the instruments. If the previous year was a black one in the history of the Band, this appeared to be gloomier. However a ray of hope was cast over the affairs by the presence in committee of the following gentlemen: Messrs. W.M. LLEWELLYN (the collieries manager), Jas. John (Plymouth and Cyfarthfa Collieries), R.M. Davies, M.E., (agent, Plymouth Collieries), ENOCH MORRELL (president, South Wales Miners' Federation), W. Morrell, B.Sc., W.M. Burrows (Co-operative Society) and J. Jones (Pontyrhun Stores). The outcome of this meeting was that Mr. W.M. Llewellyn became guarantor to Lloyd's Bank for the sum of £250 at 6% per annum. This loan enabled the Band to settle the bill of Messrs. Hawkes and Son.

At the same meeting Mr. W.M. Llewellyn particularly stressed the desirability of the workmen at the collieries resuming their weekly contributions, that collections should be made regularly at Band meetings, etc., on Friday evenings, and that tradespeople should become more interested in promoting the welfare of the Troedyrhiw Band by offering greater assistance than had hitherto been given. The New Hall, Pentrebach, was generously placed at the Band's disposal.

In the summer of 1927 the Labour Club, Dowlais, was opened, Troedyrhiw Band taking a prominent part in the ceremony.

The patients and staff of the Merthyr General Hospital were entertained on all possible occasions throughout the season.

A DEPUTATION TO W.M. LLEWELLYN

Trade depression continued to affect the business of the coal-field, many of the Band members had become unemployed in consequence, and the outlook, generally speaking, appeared other than rosy for all concerned. So bad, indeed, were conditions that a deputation of bandsmen waited upon Mr. W.M. Llewellyn, and the situation became somewhat easier. A few of the boys were given work, while arrangements were obligingly made so that all of the personnel of the Band found it possible to attend practice meetings, and any functions otherwise promoted by and for the instrumentalists.

BAND UNIFORMS PROCURED

This grievous matter thus settled fairly satisfactorily, elbow room was available, and uniforms were considered desirable. The Merthyr Vale Band was defunct, so tunics were available cheaply. Mr. Tom Owen supplied the necessary tailoring for needed alterations. Thus the Band was suitably clothed for its attendance at the parade of the Ambulance Brigade, afterwards being photographed by Mr. George Fereday (by the kind permission of Mr. James Johns), in the grounds of Pentrebach Villa.

CRYSTAL PALACE VISIT

In order to raise funds to attend the Band Contest at Crystal Palace, a prize drawing was indulged in, with excellent results. The visit to Crystal Palace materialised. Troedyrhiw Town Silver Band was one of twenty four contestants. The test piece was "Cosi Fan Tutte", and the Troedyrhiw Band was fifteenth taking the platform to play for the B Bands Challenge Shield. Thus the adjudication: Messrs. Maurice Johnstone and Basil Windsor, the adjudicators said: Number Fifteen (Troedyrhiw) Andante: "A good sonorous opening and beautiful solo playing. A little untunefulness creeps in. A nice flugel is heard, beautiful expression is shown; hope you keep it up. Presto: Nice useful speed and very acceptable inside accompaniments. Good, bright tone in the tuttis; good balance displayed. Trombones too loud in the accompaniment. Flexible technique given. A good band with all the attributes of good playing, keeping well together, although the trombones are too predominant they approach the climax splendidly. The grace notes were clearly heard without the jumbling as given by some bands. There was a tendency here and there to hurry but you came through quite all right. The opening movements and the general correctness of playing in the presto, combined with good tone and tune, made you the best band".

BAND'S PERFORMANCE REVIEWED.

I may be justifiably excused for using the following references to the above performance, culled from the "British Bandsman": "I just managed to catch Troedyrhiw Band going on in the Junior Shield B contest. From the tootle of the first note to the end of the last, here was a rendering that in spite of an entry of twenty seven from large and small English towns, I felt confident that this - the only Welsh Band - had given them all something to sit up to, and evidently the judge found it to be so.

Troedyrhiw (meaning the foot of the slope) have thus belied the origin of their name. Today they are the proud holders of the Fifty Guinea "Isles" Challenge Shield, and are the champions of their class in Great Britain. How is that compared with those of the 'onion patch' known as the South Wales Association area. Troedyrhiw Band are not members of the said Association, and we are justified in saying that, having refused to be spoon-fed on associations, musical sops, they struck the sensible idea of providing their own diet, and thus today find themselves grown into little giants of whom Wales generally is proud. Here's to you all at Top-y-rhiw --- Garth-owen".

Again: "South Wales. Bravo,Troedyrhiw; well done! You have saved Wales, for you were the only band to bring back the cash spoils from the Crystal Palace, and that a first, too". Cymro. (*Merthyr Express.* 12.12.1931.p.8.)

It will be readily understood that there was great jubilation in the town when the news of Troedyrhiw Band's achievement at Crystal Palace spread through the streets, and the greeting it received on its return to Troedyrhiw is beyond description. The welcome was not altogether undeserved, as the bringing home of the Junior Shield meant much preparation and careful training, the resultant renown giving to Troedyrhiw a special niche in the musical firmament.

The revelry attained its zenith on 18th. October, when Mrs. Brown, of the Masons' Arms, gave her Hallowe'en dinner as a mark of appreciation of the Band's success in having its name inscribed on so well-known a trophy as the "Isles" B Bands' Challenge Shield.

SUNDAY EVENTS 1927

The 12th. November was Mayor's Sunday at Troedyrhiw, Mrs. M.A. EDMUNDS, J.P., term of office. The Troedyrhiw Band led the procession to St. John's Church for morning service. Later the Mayor addressed a meeting at the Boys' School.

At Aberfan, the following Sunday, the band was appointed to lead the procession, which marched from the Boys' School to the Recreation Ground, where the EARL OF PLYMOUTH unveiled the War Memorial to the fallen heroes of Merthyr Vale and Aberfan.

A year of strenuous endeavour was suitably ended by the success of the annual prize drawing to the great delight of all concerned.

SACRED CONCERT, DEML, ABERCANNAID, 1928

Troedyrhiw Band gave their services in aid of charity in February 1928. The Troedyrhiw (General Hospital) Fete and Gala Committee held a sacred concert on 12th. February at Deml Baptist Chapel, Abercannaid, Mrs. James Johns, Pentrebach Villa, presiding. That favourite tune "Cwm Rhondda" closed a pleasant musical night, the chairman and Mr. Aneurin Morgan expressing thanks for services, the audience heartily concurring. Congratulations were sent by the committee to Councillor Lewis M. Jones and Mr.W. Burrows on their elevation to the magisterial bench of the Borough. Sad to relate, within a fortnight of recording the above felicitations, Mr. Burrows passed away after a brief illness.

THREE MUSICAL EVENTS 1928

On the 17th. March, the Band's playing in the grounds of the Merthyr General Hospital entertained the patients and staff, afterwards marching and playing through the town.

On 22nd. March a benefit concert was given, assisted by the Troedyrhiw Ladies Choir, Miss Kate Roberts conductress, when renderings by Choir and Band were highly appreciated. On this occasion Mr. Glyn Francis (trombonist) gave the "Tyroline" solo, and Mr. Emlyn Francis the horn solo "My Pretty Jane". Mr. G.E. Brown, Headmaster, Troedyrhiw Boys' School, presided.

The concert arranged by the Ladies' Committee took place on 24th. March, the Mayor, Councillor Mrs. M.A. Edmunds, J.P., presiding, supported by Councillor Enoch Morrell. Mrs. Morrell (chairman of committee) brought National Eisteddfod winners to grace the platform.

ELECTION OF OFFICERS, 1928

At the Masons' Arms on 25th. March, a meeting was convened for the election of officers and committee. The following were chosen: Chairman, Mr. J. Williams; treasurer, Mr. Victor Ford; secretary, Mr. William Jones; committee, Messrs. Wm. Griffiths, Aaron Bulford, John Davies, W.J. Davies, Gladstone Jones, W. Morgan (Treharris), John Lewis (head teacher), Jerry Flynn, Tom Rees (Pentrebach), Reggie Brown, illegible, and Edward Chamberlain, D.C.M.

Mr. Joseph Williams, bandmaster, presented a medal to each of the playing members of the Band, a memento of the Crystal Palace success. At the same meeting the Bandmaster was directed to enquire into the matter of an invitation received from the B.B.C. Station, Cardiff.

DRAMA PRESENTED

The drama, "Brown Sugar", was presented at the New Hall, Pentrebach, proceeds in aid of the Band, on 5th. April 1928. The venture was a success, Mr. W. Richards being the producer, while Mr. W.J. Jones, M.E., Plymouth Collieries, presided. Next evening Messrs. W. and T. Williams gave a box of cigarettes to be raffled, so as to provide funds for the unemployed bandsmen who were going to the band contest at Kerne Bridge (Hereford and Worcester) the following day.

Thanks were heartily returned to the Tabernacle Church for their kindness in loaning the Hall to the Band for a concert. This was the first concert that the Band had attended dressed in uniform. There were ten bands in the competition, and the Troedyrhiw Band was fifth in order of merit, Mr. Mercer, the adjudicator saying that but a few points separated the first five bands.

Mr. W. Gibbon, Double "B" player, was compelled to resign owing to ill-health. He was an earnest, capable and faithful member, and the Band, recognising this, sent him a letter of sympathy expressing regret that his illness was the loss of the services of so good a player. Mr. Charles Addiscot, another bandsman of inestimable worth, at this time, suffered a sad bereavement by the death of his wife. Condolence was expressed and conveyed to the sorrowing member and family, as well as an inscribed wreath as a tribute and mark of respect.

MISCELLANEOUS FUND RAISING, 1928

Funds being low collections were resorted to. Messrs. J. Williams and J. Davies, by their efforts, realised £1..12s.

On 5th. May, the day of the local Miners' Road Race, the Band turned out, and the industry of the committee men with their collecting boxes produced 19s. Mr. Scarrott, the showman, kindly gave a benefit, the amount earned being 16s. Lord Buckland sent

86

£2..2s. donation; shortly after the receipt of this sum the sad news of his lordship's fatal accident reached the town. The Band conveyed its condolence to Lady Buckland and family. Mr. W. Watkins lent £5 to the Band's exchequer, for which he was thanked.

The Bandmaster, with a few members, went to Cardiff to assist the CWM BAND, Ebbw Vale, at the Miners' Road Race, the Troedyrhiw Bandmaster conducting the Cwm Band.

The next project of the Band was to promote a charity dance in aid of Mr. T.J. Grant, one of its members who had been seriously ill. The Band attended the dance, which was a huge success.

SUNDAY CONCERTS

At the Cinema, Aberfan, the MERTHYR VALE AND DISTRICT DRUM AND FIFE BAND organised a highly successful Sunday evening concert. The building was loaned for the occasion. In an ambitious programme the Troedyrhiw Town Silver Band was assisted by the vocalists, Miss W. Harris (Aberfan) and Mr.E. Morgan (Troedyrhiw). Mr. D. Williams (Troedyrhiw) was accompanist, while Alderman David Jones, Merthyr Vale, presided.

On Whit-Sunday night an open air concert was held on the Sewer Farm Field, when a large crowd was entertained. Among other items of interest, the test pieces for the Cyfarthfa and Pontypridd band contests were played.

Whit-Tuesday, the occasion of the Hospital Fete and Gala band contest, the Troedyrhiw Band came second in the march and third in the test piece "Mirella". Mr. Fred Wade was adjudicator. The following day, at Pontypridd, in the brass band contest promoted by the South Wales and Monmouthshire Bands' Association, adjudicator Mr. G. Nicholls, Sheffield, the Troedyrhiw Band repeated the performance of the Cyfarthfa Park contest, coming second and third in march and test piece respectively.

SATURDAY EVENTS

The exchequer being still short, local tradespeople were visited, and the sum of £1..10s. accrued from these calls. On the same day, 2nd. June, the Band presented itself at the Pentrebach Cricket Ground, where a match was in progress between Hill's Plymouth and Brecon, later parading the streets of Pentrebach.

Saturday 16th. June, the date of the annual parade and inspection of the Merthyr Tydfil area of the St. John Ambulance Brigade, Troedyrhiw Band was engaged to head the procession from the Grove to Aberfan-road, Perthigleision, Bryngoleu-lane, and on to the Coffee Tavern Field, where the inspection by Colonel Lewis, Cardiff, took place. Appreciation was expressed for the kind services of the Band.

OBITUARIES

Here is recorded the demise of Mr. ROBERT OWEN, last of the brothers of Councillor Mrs. M.A. EDMUNDS, J.P., who died in London. The Band extended its sympathies to the bereaved lady.

Again it is noted that by the death of Mr. T.J. Grant another good bandsman has gone from our ranks. The usual condolences were sent to the sorrowing mother as well as a wreath, a tribute from Mr. Grant's fellow bandsmen. The funeral took place on Thursday 21st. June. It was headed by the Band and was attended by a large concourse of mourners, friends and sympathisers. The streets along the route to the Cemetery, Aberfan, were dense with onlookers, the Band meanwhile playing the "Dead March" (Saul). At the house the hymn tunes, "Rhondda" and "Guide me, O Thou Great Jehovah" were rendered, and at the graveside were played "Aberystwyth" and "Jesu, Lover of My Soul". Officers and committee-men were chosen bearers for their departed comrade.

SUMMER OUTINGS

On 30th. June the Troedyrhiw Band contested the Caerphilly band contest, both in Class B and C. Mr. Eastwood, Birmingham, was the adjudicator. He highly praised the performance, specially mentioning Mr. Glyn Francis, "G" trombonist, and Mr. Matthew Williams, the cornet soloist.

A garden party, given at Llwydcoed, in aid of the Nursing Home, Aberdare, was attended by the Band, and the visitors were pleasantly entertained. The programme consisted of "Poet and Peasant", selections from "Maritana", "Reminiscences of Wales", "A Day with the Huntsmen", "Selections from Verdi", "Musical Fragments", "Mephistopheles", "B.B. and C.F. March", and "Ar Hyd y Nos". In the evening there was dancing on the green, to the accompaniment of the Band.

On 28th. July 1928 the Welfare Recreation Ground, The Willows, was officially opened by the Mayor, Councillor Mrs. M.A. Edmunds, J.P.. Among the guests were Councillor E. Morrell, J.P., Mr. Griffith Llewellyn, (solicitor), Mr. James Johns (Plymouth and Cyfarthfa Collieries), and Mr. R.L. Davies, M.I.M.E. (agent, Plymouth Collieries), the Band being in attendance for the day. (*Merthyr Express*. 26.12.1931.)

EISTEDDFOD, NEW HALL, PENTREBACH, 1931.

Troedyrhiw Town Silver Band promoted an eisteddfod on a big scale on Saturday 20th. June 1931, and, so far as can be gathered, intended to make it an annual feature. The venture was staged at the New Hall, Pentrebach. The explanation for such venue is made in the letter quoted here, vide the *Merthyr Express*, 6th. June 1931:

Troedyrhiw Band Eisteddfod

Sir, We trust you will grant us a little space and insert this letter explaining why the Troedyrhiw Band are holding their eisteddfod at the New Hall, Pentrebach.

We have made untiring efforts, through different channels, to obtain the St. John's Hall, Troedyrhiw, but failed, as St. John's Hall could not be granted for a Saturday.

Anyone familiar with the holding of an eisteddfod on a scale similar to this one will certainly agree that a day other than Saturday would not be suitable, when one considers the number of items allocated for children and the difficulty of male voice choirs, as members of same may be working afternoon and night shifts.

Troedyrhiw is as progressive a village as any in south Wales in every phase of life - be it music, sport or whatnot - but it is seriously handicapped by the lack of a public hall. Nevertheless we trust that the general public will rally round us so as to make the venture a success. If this be so, we intend embarking on a larger scale still, with every probability of the function taking place in Troedyrhiw, ie. in a large marquee, so that the inflow of visitors may, for one day at any rate, be of some assistance to our hard-hit tradespeople. Thanking you in anticipation, Yours, The Troedyrhiw Band Eisteddfod Committee.

88

The eisteddfod duly functioned and that very successfully. The adjudicators were Messrs. D. Williams (Treharris) and B. Griffiths (Merthyr), MUSIC; and Lewis Davies (Lewys Glan Cynon), LITERATURE. Messrs Gwilym Lewis (Merthyr) and David Williams (Troedyrhiw) were the accompanists. The eisteddfod conductor was Mr. David Francis, M.E., (Troedyrhiw); Messrs. J. Williams, W.J. Jones, J. Davies, W. Rowlands and Victor Ford being chairman, secretaries and treasurer to the committee.

The order of merit in the choral competition was as follows:
Deep Duffryn, Mountain Ash (90); Tylorstown (89); Merthyr Labour Club (85), Trelewis (85); and Troedyrhiw (83). Herewith I submit a list of donors and donations towards the above-mentioned eisteddfod:

£2..2s.0d. Mr. W.M. Llewellyn.

£1..12s..6d. Mr. Stanley Jones, Newport.

£0..10s..6d. Lord Camrose; Sir Gomer Berry; Messrs. Franklyn Davy; Parr, Rhymney; T. Jones; Goring Thomas; Wills, Bristol; E. Davies, Co-operative Society, Troedyrhiw; Ex-Servicemen's Club, Troedyrhiw; Pentrebach Workmen's Club.

£0..10s..0d. Lady Buckland, Councillor E. Morrell, C.B.E.

£0..7s..6d. Councillor Mrs. M.A. Edmunds, Mr. J. John.

£0..5s..0d. Vicar of Troedyrhiw; D.J. Jones; J.V. Williams; Harris Morris; E. Phillips; J. Jones; W.P. Morrell; James Evans; Mrs. Morgan; Messrs. Thomas and Evans; R.L. Davies; D.J. Lewis, Fernbank; W.Hale; Teachers, Boys' School, Troedyrhiw; Dr. Ferguson; S. Price; Charles Jones.

£0..3s..0d. Mr. J. Lewis.

£0..2s..6d. Messrs. Pesci Brothers; A.G. Davies; Miss Evans; H. Bland; Dr. Watkins; C. Price; W.L. Williams; G.B. Jones; Messrs. Beedle and Stephens.

£0..2s..0d. R.T. Lloyd; B.M. Davies; B.M.; Leslie Davies; R. Hopkins; H. Sleeman; Idris Jones; G. Robbins.

£0..1s..0d. Mrs. Baynham; D.J.O.; D.J. Picton; E.T. Jones; G. Jones; J. Smith; Mrs. Mahoney; Mrs. Morgan, Royal Oak; J. Bell.

£0..0s..6d. W. James.

The Band attended the 1931 annual parade of the Troedyrhiw Branch of the British Legion, the service was conducted by the Vicar. Major D. Cope Harris also addressed the throng.

On Thursday 9th. July 1931 the Hon. Mrs. J. Bruce performed the opening ceremony for the fete promoted by the Merthyr District Nursing Association, the Band was present on this occasion, with its usual repertoire of music.

To enable the Band to go to the Crystal Palace Band Contests, concerts were promoted at Troedyrhiw, Abercannaid, and Pentrebach. All were well patronised, satisfactory programmes were meted out, and the requisite wherewithal (money) was forthcoming. The Band failed to find favour with the adjudicators at the Crystal Palace in 1931, better luck next time!

Troedyrhiw Town Silver Band, in Dame Nature's way, continued to lose its members and friends. Bandsman H. Grant was bereaved of his wife; Dr. Ferguson of his son in a motorcycle accident; and Mr. E. Tovey, Wyndham-street, Troedyrhiw, some time chairman of the Band. Condolences were expressed at the meetings and conveyed to all sorrowing relatives in each case.

On 28th. September 1931 the Earl of Plymouth presented the freehold deeds of the Welfare Grounds to the Troedyrhiw Welfare Association. In the evening a presentation tea was partaken of, when Mr. Griffith Llewellyn, solicitor, presented to the secretary of the Welfare Association, Mr. Morgan, Brynawelon, in recognition of ten year's faithful service, a fine oak bookcase and bureau. The Band supplied the musical entertainment.

The Shopping Week of 1931, probably the big feature in Councillor John Williams's mayoralty tenure, kept the Band busily employed.

Remembrance Day was kept this year with the same zeal as on all previous occasions. Duty found the Band in harness both at Merthyr Vale and Troedyrhiw.

High-street Baptist Chapel, Merthyr, was the scene of the Mayoral Divine Service, on behalf of His Worship, Councillor J.E. Jones, Town Ward, the Revd. E. Ebrard Rees officiating. As hitherto, the Band headed the procession. The Chief Constable was marshal.

Through ill-health Mr. W.J. Jones resigned the Band secretaryship in August 1931, and was succeeded by Mr. W.E. Rowlands, who, in turn, vacated the post on the 29th. ult., having found employment away from home. The services of both these gentlemen were gratefully acknowledged.

The eleventh annual prize drawing on 22nd. December 1931 was a success, the benefits going to the funds of the Band.

The benefit football match, Troedyrhiw Welfare V Merthyr Town, on the Welfare Ground, took place on 28th. December. Thanks were accorded to all concerned in this matter, especially to Mr. H. Hadley, Mr. Small (referee) and Mr. Fred Bristow (Welfare secretary).

1932 opens with a cheerful note. One of our vice-presidents, Councillor E. Morrell, J.P., appeared in the King's New Year's Honours' List with a C.B.E. May this be a good omen for all of us!

In concluding these four articles, I would like to thank the Editor of the *Merthyr Express* for his kind indulgence, he being not the least of the Troedyrhiw Band's well wishers.

(*Merthyr Express.* 23.1.1932.p.8.col.1+2.)

ADDITIONAL BAND HISTORY, 1925, 1933, 1936, 1937 AND 1939

06.06.1925.   The Silver Band is adding to its record of successes, having taken two seconds at the open contest at Ross on Wye on Monday last. The adjudicator was   Mr. Brier, Blackpool. (His adjudication and lengthy comments were published but are now omitted). The Band play at St. John's Hall, Troedyrhiw, on Monday next, assisted by Miss Blodwen Owen, Treharris; Mr. Rhys Thomas and Mr. Jack Williams, Mountain Ash. (*Merthyr Express.* 6.6.1925.p.14.col.2.)

13.06.1925.   A grand concert was held at St. John's Hall on Monday evening last under the auspices of the Band, when the inhabitants of Troedyrhiw had the pleasure of hearing

such class artistes as Miss Blodwen Owen, Treharris; Mr. Rhys Thomas and Mr. Jack Williams, of Mountain Ash, ably assisted by the Band, under the conductorship of Mr. Joe Williams, the bandmaster. The Band opened the programme with the march 'Mephistopheles', followed by the test piece at Ross on Whit Monday, 'The Echoes of the Opera'. Mr. Rhys Thomas then sang 'Deeper and Deeper Still' which was encored. In response he sang 'Maid of the Mill'. Mr. J. Williams was at his best in 'Comrade', a song which drew much applause from the audience. Miss Blodwen Owen, new to Troedyrhiw concert goers, left a marked impression. A very pleasing contralto of beautiful demeanour, she sang her songs, which were of varied character, with much intelligence. 'Keep your toys, laddie boy' and 'The Glory of the Sea' were items that will be long remembered. Miss Owen and Mr. Rhys Thomas sang the duet 'Watchman, what of the Night?' and Messrs. Thomas and Williams sang 'Mae Cymru'n Barod'. 'Sincerity' by Mr. Rhys Thomas and, by request, 'The Desert' were much appreciated. 'Hallelujah Chorus', 'Euryanthe' and 'Welsh Melodies' were played well by the Band. Mr. T. Sims presided. The usual vote of thanks was proposed by Coun. Enoch Morrell, J.P., and the Chairman, in a few well chosen words, responded. Mr. David Williams, son of the conductor, was the accompanist. He was personally thanked by Mr. John Williams for his manner of playing. 'Hen Wlad fy Nhadau', sung by Miss Owen, brought to a close a most enjoyable evening.
(*Merthyr Express.* 13.6.1925.p.15.col.3.)

11.07.1925.   Co-Operators' Day. On Saturday Co-Operators' Day was celebrated in over eighty countries, the purpose of which was to call public attention to the power of co-operation in promoting the welfare of mankind. A free tea and sports was held for all members' children at the Farm Field, Troedyrhiw. The procession was headed by the local Town Band (National Eisteddfod winner), conducted by Mr. Joe Williams. Officials and two thousand children proceeded through the main streets to Troedyrhiw Farm Field where tea and cakes had been prepared. Sports followed, besides running competitions, there was a boot cleaning competition for boys and a spoon cleaning competition for girls. (Winners and judges are listed).
(*Merthyr Express.* 11.7.1925.p.15.col.3.)

01.08.1925.   The thirty seventh annual band contests of the South Wales and Monmouthshire Brass Band Association were held at Caerphilly Castle on Saturday in conjunction with the annual choral and ambulance competitions promoted by the Caerphilly Town Silver Band. Ideal weather conditions prevailed and there was a large attendance. A feature of the event was the numerous entries in the ambulance section. The proceeds will be equally divided between the Town Silver Band and the Caerphilly Workmen's Hall and Institute. Four bands entered the Class B band contest, the test piece was 'Der-Wildschutz'. The prizes were: 1, S.W. & Mon. Association Shield, silver cup and £10; 2, £4; 3, £2. The awards were: -- 1. Oakdale, Mon. (conductor Mr. H. Hayes); 2. Cwmaman (Mr. R.S. Howells); 3. Troedyrhiw (Mr. J. Williams). 4. Nantymoel (Mr. William Smith). &c. (*Merthyr Express.* 1.8.1925.p.16. col.4.)

08.08.1925.   At The Willows, Troedyrhiw, on Thursday, under the auspices of the Troedyrhiw Town Silver Band, successful sports were held. The weather proved very favourable and a large number gathered to witness the various events. The officials were : -- President, Mr.T.J. Simms, M.E.; vice presidents, Messrs W.P. Burrows, W. Herd, W. Walsh, Tom Matthews, T.L. Page and Alderman E. Morrell. J.P. Judges, Messrs. D. Francis, D.J. Picton, W. Walsh, W. Harris, Charles Woodward, W. Arnott and W.P. Burrows. Handicappers, Messrs. Harry Woodward and Glad. Jones. Starter, Mr. George Richards. Etc..

The Troedyrhiw Band, under the conductorship of Mr. Joe Williams, was in attendance and played the following excellent programme : -- 'Mephistopheles', 'Poet and Peasant', 'Der Wildshutz', 'A Day with the Huntsmen'. Concert Waltz 'Queen of the Dance', 'Echoes of the Opera', 'Tancredi', 'I Puritani' and other dance music, during which many indulged in dancing on the spacious ground. (*Merthyr Express.* 8.8.1925.p.6.col.3.)

10.10.1925.   Troedyrhiw Town Prize Band attended the great Crystal Palace contest on Saturday last and secured fifth prize, thirty one bands competed. This is surely a great feat for a young band, and Troedyrhiw should be proud of it. Great credit is due to Mr. J. Williams (hon. conductor) for the wonderful progress the Band has made since its inception in 1920. (The adjudicator's remarks were also published, these were very encouraging.)
(*Merthyr Express.* 10.10.1925.p.15.col.4.)

19.08.1933.   Obituary for Mr. E.T. Leyshon, 17, Park Place, Troedyrhiw. He was
                associated with 'Old' and 'New' Troedyrhiw Band.
                (*Merthyr Express.* 19.8.1933.p.10.col.2.)

29.02.1936   The Troedyrhiw Town Band under the conductorship of Mr. Joe Williams is busy preparing for the competitions at the band festival shortly to be held at Pontypridd.
(*Merthyr Express.* 29.2.1936.p.14.col.3.)

14.03.1936 Band success. Troedyrhiw Town Band under Mr. Joseph Williams did well at the bands' festival on Saturday at Pontypridd. They were one of eight bands in Class "C" competition and they gained first prize and cup. The bands were allowed their own selection and "Halevy" was selected by Troedyrhiw Town Band. *The committee appeals to the public for increased support,* in their efforts to maintain the high standards of the band. (*Merthyr Express.* 14.3.1936.p.10.col.1.)

16.05.1936.   Band concert. On Sunday a concert was held at the New Hall, Pentrebach, under the auspices of Troedyrhiw Town Band, conductor Mr. Joe Williams. The band gave several selections including the test piece that won them the Pontypridd Festival cup and prize. They were supported by Madam Price (Porth) and Master J. Virgin. The accompanist was Mr. David Williams. *The Band appeals to the public for their support ,* in view of the competition for which they have entered at Llandovery on Whit Monday. Mr. Rees Davies presided. Mr. Jeffries was the organising secretary. (*Merthyr Express.* Saturday. 16.5.1936.p.7.col.4.)

06.06.1936. Band's Success. The Troedyrhiw Town Band, conductor Mr. Joe Williams, was awarded the first prize at the band contest held on Whit Monday at Llandovery. The Band will again compete in the near future at Aberdare and also at Rhymney, where they hope to secure the "Daily Herald" Challenge Cup. On Sunday evening at the Lido they rendered a programme and played two test pieces. (*Merthyr Express.* 6.6.1936.p.10.col.3.)

08.08.1936. Band's success. The Troedyrhiw Town Band was awarded, at the Rhymney Hospital Fete last Saturday, the first prize in the march and first prize in the test selection, with a silver cup for the conductor Mr. Joe Williams. Medals were also secured for Mr. Tom Williams (euphonium soloist) and Mr. Matt Williams (cornet). (*Merthyr Express.* Saturday. 8.8.1936.p.11.col.4.)

29.08.1936. The Troedyrhiw Town Band under the leadership of Mr. Joseph Williams was again successful when in competition with eight other bands at Whitchurch Hospital fete and band contest on Saturday. The adjudicators complimented the Band on the excellence of their performances and awarded them the first prize in the march, first prize in the selection and the Association Challenge Cup Shield and twenty six medals. On their return home the members were given a warm reception. *The committee appeals to the general public for more generous support.* The organising secretary is Mr. A. Jeffries, Carlton-terrace. (*Merthyr Express.* 29.8.1936.p.14.col.4.)

05.09.1936. Band's success. Troedyrhiw Town Band, conductor Mr. Joe Williams, gained the first prize in the march and third in the selection competition at Oakdale Workmen's fete and gala on Saturday. (*Merthyr Express.* Saturday. 5.9.1936.p.9.col.4.)

26.09.1936. The Troedyrhiw Town Band under the leadership of Mr. Joe Williams, was again successful when in competition with six other bands, at Hirwaun sports and band contest last Saturday, the band was awarded first prize in the march and third in the selection. The organising secretary was Mr. A. Jeffries, Carlton-terrace. (*Merthyr Express.* 26.9.1936.p.11.col.4.)

10.10.1936. Troedyrhiw Town Silver Band to broadcast for the first time, courtesy of the B.B.C. Idris Daniels, baritone, is by now (1936) well known to listeners. He is singing in a concert with the Troedyrhiw Silver Band, conducted by Mr. Joe Williams, on 16th. October 1936. This is the first time that the Troedyrhiw Silver Band has appeared before the microphone. (*Merthyr Express.* 10.10.1936.p.9.col.3.)

17.10.1936. Band activities. The Band has done exceptionally well this season. On Wednesday at the Welfare Pavilion the band gave a concert, assisted by the following artistes: Miss Enid James, Mr. Dai Carston, and Master Jacky Virgin. Mr. David Williams was the accompanist and Mr. R.D. Price presided. (*Merthyr Express.* 17.10.1936.p.14.col.3.)

21.11.1936.   Marchers return. The Troedyrhiw men who took part in the recent protest march against the Means Test were met at the outskirts of the town by a large crowd, and headed by the Troedyrhiw Town Band, marched in procession along the main Cardiff-road.

A short stay was made near the Labour Club, when Mr. Harry Lucas (Chairman of the Plymouth Ward Committee) congratulated them on their sacrifice and on their exemplary conduct. Mr. W. Rowlands, the secretary, who was one of the marchers, enumerated some of their experiences. (*Merthyr Express*. 21.11.1936.p.14.col.3.)

19.06.1937.   Band Concert. Troedyrhiw Silver Band gave a programme of music, which included the test piece for the National Eisteddfod, at the Sewage Farm, on Sunday. The organising secretary was Mr. A.E. Jeffries. (*Merthyr Express*. 19.6.1937.p.11.col.3.)

03.07.1937.   The Troedyrhiw Town Band, having entered the second class contest at the National Eisteddfod, are busy rehearsing the test pieces, and to meet the expense are *appealing to the general public for their support.* The conductor is Mr. Joe Williams and the organising secretary Mr. A. Jeffries. (*Merthyr Express*. Saturday. 3.7.1937.p.14.col.4.)

18.09.1937.   Town Band. Under their NEW CONDUCTOR, Mr. Emlyn Francis, who is a member of the B.B.C. Welsh Orchestra, the Troedyrhiw Town Band is busy rehearsing in preparation for the class B championship contest at Hirwaun Eisteddfod on Saturday. (*Merthyr Express*. Saturday.18.9.1937.p.16.col.3.)

01.07.1939.   On the air. Mr. A.E. Jeffries (secretary of the Troedyrhiw and District Powell Duffryn Silver Band) has been invited to make arrangements for a broadcast programme to take place on Sunday next at four o'clock at the Pentrebach New Hall. (*Merthyr Express*. Saturday. 1.7.1939.p.15.)

12.08.1939.   Concert Rondo. Mr. Emlyn Francis was "on the air" on Monday morning last when he gave a recital. Mr. Francis is the principal horn player in the Cardiff B.B.C. Orchestra, and was formerly a member of the Troedyrhiw Town Band. (*Merthyr Express*. 12.8.1939.p.9.)

APPENDIX ONE
SOME MEMBERS, TROEDYRHIW TOWN SILVER BAND, 1952
EX. DAILY HERALD NATIONAL REGISTER OF BRASS BANDSMEN

NAME	REGISTRATION NUMBER
Brewer, F.	2/8803/46
Bulford, A.	2/8794/46
Bulford, D	4/36559/52
Bulford, June	4/36552/52
Burns, G.	4/36558/52
Connick, E.	4/36550/52
Dean, T.	4/36553/52
Ford, G.	2/8790/46
Foster, B.R.	2/8812/46
Galeozzie, T.	4/36531/52
Galeozzie, W.	4/36554/52
Jones, C.	2/8806/46
Long, D.	2/8796/46
Loveday, Thomas	4/24931/49
McCarthy, C.	4/36556/52
Morgan, G.A.	2/8795/52
Roberts, R. (Bob)	4/36557/52
Roper, Leslie	2/8801/46
Williams, G.	2/8792/46
Williams, M.	2/8791/46
Williams, T.D.	4/36555/52

"Daily Herald" National Register of Brass Bandsmen

Administrative Offices :

NATIONAL BRASS BAND CLUB REGISTRY

15, WEST STREET, LONDON, W.C. 2.

Telephone TEMple Bar 9700

The Secretary,

_____ *Troedyrhiw Silver* _____ Band

On checking your *Application for Registration Form*, I find the following bandsman is registered in the National Registry as a member of

_____ *Dowlais Silver.* _____ Band

Name of Bandsman _____

Under Rule 12 of the *National Brass Band Contesting Rules*, the transfer CANNOT be completed until I receive:-

    (a) A letter from his previous band agreeing to the transfer.

    (b) His Registration Card for endorsement.

    (c) A letter from the bandsman saying he wishes to transfer to your band.

1. This transfer MUST be completed weeks before your *Area Qualifying Contest* if you require the bandsman's services on that occasion.

2. This transfer CANNOT become effective in time for the bandsman to play with your band at the *Area Qualifying Contest*, unless authorised under Change of Residence or Employment clause.

Yours sincerely,

S. A. GRIFFIN.

Registrar.

1, Nantygwenith St
Georgetown
Merthyr.

National Registry.
'Daily Herald'

Dear Sirs.

We wish to inform you that we are authorising the transfer to Troedyrhiw Silver Band, the following bandsmen.

M. Williams. G. Williams
A. Bufford L. Rope
and. B. Foster.

We regret that we are not in possession of their registration cards. Trusting this will assist any difficulties

Yours. Faithfully,
Mr Tudor. Jones.

DOWLAIS
Secretary
SILVER BAND

DAILY HERALD

Registration No.

2/8791/46

NATIONAL BRASS BAND CHAMPIONSHIPS
OF GREAT BRITAIN
BANDSMAN'S REGISTRATION CARD

This Certifies that

M. WILLIAMS

is a registered member of

DOWLAIS SILVER BAND.

Date of Registration 27.3.46.

I, the undersigned, have read the Rules and Conditions and agree
to be bound by them in every respect.

Signature of Holder

This Registration Card is not valid unless signed by the Bandsman

DAILY HERALD

Registration No.

2/8812/46

NATIONAL BRASS BAND CHAMPIONSHIPS
OF GREAT BRITAIN
BANDSMAN'S REGISTRATION CARD

This Certifies that

B. R. FOSTER

is a registered member of

DOWLAIS SILVER BAND

Date of Registration 27.3.46.

I, the undersigned, have read the Rules and Conditions and agree
to be bound by them in every respect.

Signature of Holder

This Registration Card is not valid unless signed by the Bandsman

Early Years

In 1850 the wife of the schoolmaster at Llangollen presented him with a son, whom they named Richard Ffoulkes, after his maternal grandfather, the Revd Richard Ffoulkes, (known by his bardic name of Silas Glan Dyfrdwy), a Baptist minister of Cefnbychan. His paternal grandfather too was a well-known Welsh Independent minister, the Revd Peter Griffiths of Llanrwst. A sister married the Revd. David Davies. Richard Ffoulkes followed in the footsteps of his grandfathers rather than his father and trained for the Baptist Ministry at the North Wales Baptist College, then based at Llangollen, thus becoming part of a ministerial dynasty so typical of the Nonconformity of the period. Whilst a student he acted as founder-secretary to the newly established Llangollen School Board.

Richard Ffoulkes was bilingual but like many of his Welsh contemporaries he went to serve an English pastorate, albeit just across Offa's Dyke, at Tarporley, Cheshire, where he was ordained in 1872. He remained there for five years before moving to Nottingham where he ministered from 1877 to 1881. During this time he acted as agent for the Liberation Society, concerned with Disestablishment. He was also well known as a Temperance speaker and was prominent in the ranks of *Cymru Fydd,* a movement founded in London in 1886 on the pattern of *Young Ireland*, working to encourage Welsh culture and for Welsh Home Rule and Disestablishment of the Church of England in Wales.

The Law

Richard Ffoulkes from his student days showed a great interest in both politics and the Law. It was no surprise there that he was called to the Bar in 1879 and practised in the Chancery division, full time from 1881 onward, though many of his friends were disappointed by his leaving the Ministry. Nonetheless he continued to serve the Baptist cause in particular and Nonconformity in general. At the Bar he became prominent as an advocate opposing the licensing of public houses. He represented the temperance party at the Welsh Sunday Closing Commission, a similar commission in the Isle of Man and the House of Lords Licensing Commission. He was an authority on Chapel trusts and was known as a powerful orator on temperance platforms. He wrote regularly to publications such as *Freeman* and *Baptist.*

According to the Census of 1881, Richard F Griffiths of 4, Gedling Grove, Nottingham, was born at Llangollen, Derby, England (sic) and was aged 31. He first married in 1874 a daughter of Joseph Aston of Brassey Green. After the death of his first wife, he married again in 1879, taking as his bride Helen, then aged 19, the daughter of Professor Goadby, of Chilwell College. There were then two children, Lizzie, aged 4, born at Tarporley, and Lois, aged 5 months, born at Nottingham. There was also a maid in the household.

Merthyr Tydfil 1888

The borough constituency of Merthyr Tydfil included that borough as well as the Cynon Valley and elected two members to the House of Commons. In 1885 and 1886 it returned unopposed its two Liberal MPs, the Revd Henry Richard, first elected in 1868 and Mr Charles Herbert James, who joined him in 1880. In 1888 by-elections had to called for both seats. First, C H James resigned and a by-election on 14 March saw the unopposed return of coal magnate, David Alfred Thomas, later Viscount Rhondda. Then came the sudden death of the other MP, the Revd Henry Richard, a Congregational Minister and Secretary of the Peace Society, who had represented the seat since 1868. The local Liberal Association had promised to choose a workingman as candidate for the next vacancy before Richard died but had gone back on its pledge, causing a great protest from Labour.

The Liberals delayed in choosing a candidate and eventually brought in Ffoulkes Griffiths, now a London barrister, who was seen as a middle class import from London. The editorial in the Liberal *Merthyr Express* of 6 October 1888 damned the new candidate with faint praise: "The die is cast. Mr. Ffoulkes Griffiths has been adopted by the Liberal associations of the borough, not because he was the best man before them – nobody pretended that – but because he was the only man left available for a pressing emergency. It was a sort of Hobson's choice – Ffoulkes Griffiths or nobody – and the Associations realising the situation before them have taken Mr. Griffiths.... Though Mr. Ffoulkes Griffiths is not for an instant to be compared with Mr. Henry Richard, or some of the other men whose names were before the Association, he is still a Liberal of pronounced views, able to give intelligent reasons for the faith that is in him, and may be relied upon to give effect by his votes to the political feeling of the great majority of the electorate of Merthyr...The South Wales Conservative daily, *The Western Mail* even more scathing: "A person named R. Ffoulkes Griffiths, of heaven knows what place, what talents or what nation has been foisted on the borough[1]." .

Ffoulkes Griffiths fought as strong a campaign as was possible. He was supported by the other MP for Merthyr Tydfil, a two-member seat, Mr. D. A. Thomas, the coal magnate and later Viscount Rhondda. Thomas would not be welcomed by the more left wing of the mining community. Griffiths' platform was orthodox Liberal. His speeches laid stress on Welsh national aspirations ("they in Wales were beginning to feel their power and they would make the English cabinet know it too. The English cabinet should know that Welshmen were born to be free (applause|)". As one might expect, the other main planks in his platform were Temperance, Disestablishment, and Irish Home Rule. There appears to have been no reference to the needs and rights of industrial workers. This would have been a difficult subject for any Liberal in an area such as Merthyr Tydfil,

---

[1] *Western Mail 5 October 1888.*

seeking the support of the workers on one side and that of D. A. Thomas and middle class Nonconformists on the other. One suspects that Griffiths thought that the votes of the Welsh-speaking miners and other industrial workers were safe for the Liberal cause.

Griffiths' opponent, William Prichard Morgan, was a maverick figure who was born at Usk in 1844, the son of a Wesleyan local preacher. He ran away to sea and returned home to a law office, qualifying as a solicitor in 1865. He went to Australia, setting up an office at the Gympie goldfield in 1867. Buying and selling gold made him a rich man. He had many legal battles with the Premier of New South Wales, Sir Samuel Griffith, a native of Merthyr Tydfil. After speculating for gold in Korea he returned to Wales, developing the Morgan Gold Mine and founding the Merioneth Gold Company. Morgan was nicknamed both *King Gold* and *The Member for China* because of his long absences prospecting for gold in that country. He was an ardent imperialist and it was alleged that he dealt in "Chinese labour". He claimed to be *The Labour Candidate* and presented himself as the local man made good. He flooded the constituency with leaflets bearing a picture of himself dressed in miners' clothes, with a naked candle in his cap though he never spoke of workers' needs and rights. Morgan received powerful backing from the brewers and licensed victuallers as well as the local Conservatives and Labour voters (especially in Aberdare) so that his election expenses of almost £1,000 proved an excellent investment. The Morgan campaign was powerful, gaining much support from working class voters by skilful attacks on both the local Liberal Association and its unfortunate candidate. It centred on two obvious weaknesses in the Liberal choice as far as the local electorate was concerned as well as on several apparent strengths.

The first weakness was the high-handed and competent behaviour of the local Liberal Association in ignoring its earlier promise to field a Labour candidate and then giving a series of mixed signals as it dithered before choosing in a last minute hurry a complete stranger to the constituency.

Then much play was made by Griffiths' opponent and his allies that the official Liberal candidate was a 'carpetbagger" and a complete stranger to the constituency (as was Morgan) and had no experience of industry. As the *Merthyr Express* reported on 13 October, "He (Mr. Morgan) was not going there (House of Commons) as a briefless barrister in the hope of gaining some appointment under the Crown but he was going there as a mining man, who had worked with his own hands, and who knew what difficulties existed in the way of enabling men to obtain a livelihood from the bowels of the earth."

The constituency, which included Aberdare as well as Merthyr Tydfil, included a large number of monoglot Welsh speaking voters who rightly expected to be addressed in their own language. Liberal Party supporters made great play of the fact that Prichard Morgan was not a Welsh speaker but that too misfired in contrast to Griffiths who was Welsh speaking and a prominent supporter of *Cymru Fydd*. Morgan launched a powerful counter-attack: "His opponent had the advantage over him of being able to speak Welsh. He admitted it to be a great advantage but it should not be such an advantage as to exclude from the House of Commons a man who was otherwise worthy of occupying the position of a Member of Parliament (hear hear). Sometimes a Welshman, even at the loss of knowing his mother tongue, might be able to do some good in the world, and he had no hesitation in saying that, not speaking Welsh, he had done as much good in the Principality as Mr. Ffoulkes Griffiths (applause). Though, however, he was unable to speak Welsh, his children were learning the language, and he himself was picking it up little by little, so that by-and-bye he would probably be competent to go to the same terrific extent as their present member, Mr. D. A. Thomas and speak a few sentences in the vernacular. (Thomas was not fluent in Welsh). They knew very well that Welsh was not spoken in the House of Commons, and the fact of Mr. Ffoulkes Griffiths' speaking it would not enhance his value in the House of Commons one jot or tittle. (applause)." At the same time the quality of Griffiths' spoken Welsh was undergoing scrutiny. The same issue of the *Merthyr Express* contained a letter in Welsh from Idris Fychan of Dowlais in which the writer expressed his disappointment in the Liberal candidate. Idris Fychan described himself as one who favoured having a Welsh-speaking candidate "but I must express my great disappointment in the person chosen. I am in no position to pass judgement on the quality of his English but can pooh-pooh the kind of Welsh he has. At the Dowlais meeting several monoglot Welshmen were shouting "Welsh, Welsh" as the speaker was speaking his own kind of Welsh, whilst they thought he was speaking a different language." Idris Fychan was sure that Prichard Morgan could do just as well if her tried and ends by saying that "What is more unforgivable from him (Griffiths) than from Mr. Prichard Morgan is that it is said that he spent three years at Llangollen College, the Baptist College, at the expense of that denomination, and that the Welsh language is used there. This clearly proves to me the truth of the article in *Y Faner*[2]- that Ffoulkes, poor thing, turned into a *Dic Sion Dafydd (Uncle Tom* figure) on reaching London; and that he has not linked himself with any Welsh institution in the capital city. Nothing is more hateful to every pure Welshman than such a character."[3]

Ffoulkes Griffiths was fighting to succeed another Nonconformist minister as MP. The Revd. Henry Richard had represented Merthyr Tydfil from 1868 until his recent death. His successor as Liberal candidate could draw strength too from his Nonconformist credentials as a former Baptist minister and the grandson of two ministers, one Baptist, the other Congregationalist. Attacks such as that made in the letter of Idris Fychan, quoted above, greatly undermined the Baptist's cause. Similarly the strong stand taken by

---

[2] *Welsh weekly newspaper*

[3] *Fel un oedd yn ffafr cael Cymro fel ymgeisydd seneddol, rhaid i mi ddweyd fy mod wedi cael fy siomi'n fawr yn yr un a gafwyd fel y cyfryw. Nis gallaf farnu llawer am ei Saesoneg ond naw wfft i'r fath Gymraeg sydd ganddo. Yn y cyfarfod yn Nowlais yr oedd amryw Cymry uniaith yn gwaeddu 'Cymraeg', tra yr oedd y dyn ar y pryd yn siarad Cymraeg, fel yr oedd ganddo ef, a hwythau yn meddwl mai rhyw iaith arall ydoedd... Y mae hyn yn fwy anfaddeuol ..o'r du ef nag o du Mr. Prichard Morgan. Oblegid dywedir ei fod wedi treulio tair blynedd yng Ngholeg Llangollen, Coleg y Bedyddwyr, ar gost yr enwad honno, ac y mae'r iaith Gymraeg yn cael ei arfer yno. Y mae hyn yn profi yn eglur i ni wirionedd yr hyn a ddywed Y Faner – mai troi yn Dic Shôn Dafydd waneth Ffoulkes, druan,wedi cyrraedd Llundain; ac na chyssylltodd ei hun ag unrhyw sefydliad Cymreig o'r y brif ddinas. Nid oes dim yn fwy atgas gan bob Cymro pur na chymeriad o'r fath.*

Griffiths on the Temperance issue provided strong ammunition to the licensed victuallers in persuading their clientele to support Morgan who at one and the same time "considered drunk a curse" (aimed at the temperance lobby) and "supported Local Option" (to please the drink trade).

Morgan turned the spotlight on Ffoulkes Griffiths career in a revealing and damaging way during the by-election campaign: 'I will tell you how he came to leave the ministry. Some time ago he wrote something and an action for libel was brought against him. He won his own case and the judge said, "This man should be wearing the wigs and gowns of those counsel.[4] This is borne out in an obituary which states that 'Whilst at Nottingham, he was brought prominently before the public as defendant in a libel case, brought against him at the instance of Mr Fred Bell, a notorious preacher of the day. The charge was a criminal one and Mr Griffiths was acquitted by the jury, and the Judge, Lord Coleridge, praised him for his action'.[5]

At the same time Morgan presented himself in a masterly way to the Nonconformists of the constituency: "Referring to the Disestablishment question, Mr. Morgan said that he was a Nonconformist and was in favour of Disestablishment. His children had also been brought up in the principles of Nonconformity - (hear, hear) – and he did not believe in a nation as a people supporting a Church in which they did not worship and in which they had no interest whatsoever." His objection to the Disendowment of the Church in the same speech would ensure that he also had Anglican votes.

There was a violent side to the election campaign, as reported in the *Merthyr Express* on 20 October. It described loud and prolonged heckling at Ffoulkes Griffiths' meeting at Cwmbach, Aberdare. There was an "Uproarious Meeting at Dowlais". Then the Liberal Party brought in Dr. Fox, Irish Nationalist M.P. for the Tullamore division of Kings County to win over the considerable Irish vote in the constituency. He addressed meetings in Merthyr and Dowlais on Sunday but was summoned back to London on Monday. The chair was taken at a crowded meeting in Dowlais on Monday evening by Mr. Mansfield, President of the Dowlais branch of the Irish National League and a motion "that we give our hearty support to the candidature of Mr. Ffoulkes Griffiths" was presented. A "running fire of interruptions from the supporters of Mr. Prichard Morgan" developed into a fight in the gallery and several people were ejected from the hall. On the following Thursday evening there was a "Disgraceful Attack on Mr. Ffoulkes Griffiths and his Friends" as he and a group of supporters walked back to Merthyr after a meeting at Cefn Coed. They were "mobbed in the road by a crowd of about one thousand persons. Sand and stones were thrown and he was violently bustled about and forced into a corner by a grocer's shop." Both candidate and police escort were showered with stones and a sergeant was struck on the back. According to Griffiths the trouble began as he left the meeting when he was jostled by a group of some fifty youths singing Prichard Morgan

---

[4] *Cambria Daily Leader 15 October 1888*
[5] *East Midland Baptist Magazine, May 1901*

songs who separated him from his companions and "seemed anxious to run me down". A number of Welshmen and Irishmen came to his rescue and formed a bodyguard. Then the crowd threw stones and sand. Lime was thrown in the face of the Revd. H. J. Hughes of Cefn Coed even though the crowd had been told who he was. Similar disturbances took place at the Temperance Hall, Aberdare, when Griffiths rose to address the meeting, Not even the presence of Tom Ellis, MP for Merioneth, quietened the opposition. All in all Griffiths was given a very rough time in the speeches and letters of his opponent and Morgan's supporters and by the rough behaviour of many in the Morgan camp, warmed into action by the largesse of the licensed victuallers. The *Western Mail* fired anti Griffiths broadsides day after day.

Polling Day was 26 October and poor Ffoulkes Griffiths was trounced by his opponent. Morgan's majority was a massive 2,193 or 18.2%. It was a humiliating defeat for both the unfortunate candidate and the local Liberal Association. The creaking Liberal organisation in Merthyr Tydfil collapsed completely and never really recovered. Poor Griffiths was sent packing, a scapegoat for Liberal Party failure.

Merthyr's Representation 1888-1900

Seven parliamentary elections were called in this constituency between1885 and 1900 though three of these were unopposed. The first Conservative candidate appeared in 1892. Benjamin Francis-Williams QC was the son of a Merthyr Baptist minister, the Revd Enoch Williams. After an education at Swansea Grammar School, Shrewsbury School and St. John's College, Cambridge, he was called to the Bar by the Middle Temple. His first wife was Willameta Hughes, daughter of a Vicar of Ebbw Vale. He had become an Anglican. He served as Recorder of Carmarthen and was Recorder of Cardiff at the time of his death in 1914.

D.A. Thomas and W. Prichard Morgan faced opposition from two directions in the next general election in 1895. The Conservatives chose a formidable local candidate in the person of Herbert Clark Lewis, son of the coal magnate, Sir William Thomas Lewis, whom he succeeded in 1914 as the 2nd Baron Merthyr. His maternal grandfather, William Rees of Aberdare was also a coal owner and a cousin to Charles Frederick Howell Green, later Bishop of Monmouth and Archbishop of Wales. Lewis' vote would suggest that he benefited from the fact of his being a local employer. Allen Upward, a banker's son, was born at Worcester. After graduating at Trinity College, Dublin, he was called to the Bar. Later he became a journalist, author and poet, and was for some time a columnist on a Merthyr newspaper. He was a member of the Gorsedd of Bards with the bardic name of Maenhir. Upward was very involved in Merthyr politics. He had planned to contest the 1892 election but withdrew his name. In 1895 he described himself as *the only Liberal (in Merthyr) candidate never to be a Tory,* showing real sympathy for the cause of working people and calling for the founding of a Labour party. His defeat in 1895 came as a great disappointment, so much so that he left Merthyr. He fought on the Greek side in the war with Turkey before spending six years as a political officer in the Colonial Service in

Nigeria. Upward suffered from periodic bouts of depression and during one such bout shot himself in the heart in January 1926. His body was discovered in his rooms at Verwood near Wimborne in Dorset.[6] David Pretty describes him as *a man of brilliant talents but with maverick tendencies.*[7]

History was made in this seat in 1900 when the electors rejected Prichard Morgan in favour of the first representative of the Independent Labour Party, James Keir Hardie. Hardie, who had grown up in great poverty, entered a Lanarkshire coalmine at the age of ten, prior to becoming Secretary of the Scottish Miners' Federation in 1886 and of the Scottish Labour Party in 1888. He contested Mid Lanarkshire twice before serving as MP for West Ham South from 1892 to 1895. His 1900 manifesto said that *my cause is the cause of Labour – the cause of humanity – the cause of God... The Nationalist Party I have in mind is this – the people of Wales fighting to recover the land of Wales...* Keir Hardie was re-elected in the next three general elections but died of a broken heart in 1915 when his beloved electors succumbed to the lure of jingoistic slogans at the outbreak of the Great War. Prichard Morgan stood unsuccessfully in Merthyr Tydfil as an Independent Liberal in January 1910 and opposed H. H. Asquith as an Independent in East Fife in 1918. He died on 5 July 1924. D A Thomas went to the House of Lords in 1910. Lloyd George appointed him President of the Board of Trade in 1916 and then Controller of Food from 1917 to the end of the War. He died in 1918.

Griffiths' Last Years

But what of Richard Ffoulkes Griffiths? For the last two years of his life, he was ill with 'paralysis' (a stroke?) and went to live with his daughter at 'Morfen', Llandudno. He was struck down for a second time on the eve of Easter Sunday and remained unconscious until his death two days later on 9 April 1901. He was buried at the cemetery of Tarporley Baptist Church, where he had been ordained nineteen years earlier. One is left wondering what his political career might have achieved had it not been for the blundering of the Liberals at Merthyr Tydfil in 1888. He happened to be a candidate in the wrong place at the wrong time. It is quite possible that he would have given good service as a typical Liberal MP of his day in other circumstances.

---

[6] *Cambrian Daily Leader, 18 January 1926*
[7] *David A Pretty, 'John Owen (ap Ffermwr) and the Labour Movement in Wales, Morgannwg XXXIII 1996.*

1885

Charles Herbert James	(Lib)	Unopposed
Revd Henry Richard	(Lib)	Unopposed

1886

Charles Herbert James	(Lib)	Unopposed
Revd Henry Richard	(Lib)	Unopposed

By-Election, 14 March 1888
On the resignation of Charles Herbert James

David Alfred Thomas	(Lib)	Unopposed

By-Election, 26 October 1888
On the death of the Revd Henry Richard

William Prichard Morgan	(Ind. Lib)	7,149	59.1%
Richard Ffoulkes Griffiths	(Lib)	4,956	40.9%
Ind.Lib. Gain		2,193	18.2%

1892

David Alfred Thomas	(Lib)	11,948	45.9%
William Prichard Morgan	(Lib)	11,756	45.2%
Benjamin Francis-Williams	(Con)	2,304	8.9%
		9,452	36.3%

1895

David Alfred Thomas	(Lib)	9,250	37.1%
William Prichard Morgan	(Lib)	8,554	34.2%
Herbert Clark Lewis	(Con)	6,525	26.1%
Allen Upward	(Ind.Lib-Lab)	659	2.6%
		2,029	8.1%

1900

David Alfred Thomas	(Lib)	8,598	46.9%
James Keir Hardie	(ILP)	5,745	31.3%
William Prichard Morgan	(Lib)	4,004	21.8%
ILP gain from Liberal		1,741	9.5%

LETTERS FROM MERTHYR TYDFIL M.P.
CHARLES HERBERT JAMES
TO HIS SISTER-IN-LAW
MARY THOMAS

The letters reproduced here were published in 1892 after the death of C.H. James, M.P. (1). They were printed by Merthyr printer, John P. Lewis, 46, High-street, M.T., son of Rhys Lewis, printer, the subject of an extended essay in *Merthyr Historian*, Volume Fourteen. The 1892 booklet was located, and forwarded to M.T. Historical Society, by Mrs. Judith Jones, M.A., Society member.

18th. July 1880.
My Dear Mary,
When I have some spare time, I may give you now and again some account of what I see or hear in Parliament, and this will while away a few minutes pleasantly, for me to write, and possibly for you to read. At some remote time in the future, you may hand over the letters to Sarah or to one of the granddaughters as a reminiscence of their grandfather.

One day we, that is the House of Commons, were summoned to the House of Lords, to hear the Royal Assent given to certain Bills which had passed both Houses. I must tell you that the House of Lords is on one side of the Palace of Westminster, and the House of Commons is on the other side, and to pass from one to the other (say from the Lords to the Commons) you traverse first a corridor with frescoes on each side, then the Great Hall, then the Hall immediately adjoining the House of Commons. Just before we were summoned I happened to be in the great Hall: I heard a row, and before I could get into the House here comes an old gentleman, the messenger from the House of Lords (the Black Rod), and walked up towards the door of the main entrance, and, as he came up, it was shut in his face by the Sergeant-at-Arms. Whereupon with his black rod, which looks like ebony tipped with gold, he knocks at the door three times, and the Sergeant opens it. Then the Black Rod marches up the floor of the House, he makes an obeisance at the bar, and then again about half way up the floor, and when he comes up near the table he stops and delivers his message, that the House of Lords desires (I think that is the word) the attendance of the House of Commons, to hear the Royal Assent given to certain Bills. I believe on one occasion this Black Rod said 'requests', or some word of that kind, and there was a great murmur and hubbub of disapprobation. Since then he has said 'desires' distinctly enough. It seems to be a rule of the House not to have any love for Mr. Black Rod. Having delivered his message he has to back out with his face to the Speaker, bowing twice as he does so till he arrives at the bar, then walks away. The first time he came to the new Parliament he sidled a little to one side before he came to the bar, as though he intended to turn before he came to the bar, at which we all murmured as though we had been cheated: since then he has been punctilious. The Speaker remains seated the whole time.

Well, Black Rod having gone, the Speaker immediately gets up, the Sergeant-at-Arms goes and shoulders the mace and walks before Mr. Speaker. Such of the members as choose go after him. For once I went. We march along, following the mace and Mr. Speaker, who of course is in wig and gown, through the Hall, then along the corridor, then across the Great Hall, then along another corridor, when we find ourselves at one end of the House of Lords, rich with carving and gold, and all the seats *scarlet* leather-work - ours are green. Mr. Speaker stands at what, I believe, is the bar of the House of Lords, with his faithful Commons behind him, having the Sergeant-at-Arms with his mace on one side of him, and Black Rod on the other.

On the woolsack sat the Chancellor with the Commissioners one on each side. At a table in the middle of the House were the Clerks of the House dressed as ordinary barristers.

The Lord Chancellor and Commissioners were in scarlet robes and hats of ancient form; the two Commissioners had long wands in their hands. From my remembrance the Lord Chancellor's hat was round, and the other Commissioners' three-cornered. Inasmuch as the Royal Assent was given by commission and not by the Queen in person, it became necessary   to show us that they had authority, so the Royal Commission was read at the table by one of the officials. When he came to the name of either of the Commissioners he stopped, made a most profound reverence, whereupon the Commissioner named took off his hat and then replaced it; then the reading went on, and at last that document was finished. The Commissioners sat; we all stood. There were a couple of jolly young girls who got into a place close by me, and, horrible to relate, while part of the performance was going on, they laughed most irreverently!! Well, the name of the Bill that was to be passed was given, and another of the officials turned towards us and repeated the words in Norman-French, accustomed on these occasions.

The business being over, Mr. Speaker makes a bow, the Sergeant shoulders the mace. He walks back, we all following, a lane being kept for us in the Hall by the police, and we see Mr. Speaker safely in his chair. The sergeant puts the mace on the table, whereby the House is constituted. He informs the House what has been done while he was away, and we begin our interminable talk once more. This which I have described happened some time ago.

On Friday we had a very exciting debate over the Prince Imperial monument, with some very peculiar incidents, when I suspect, you will have to refer to my plan, when I describe them, which I hope to do some day, as some queer customs of the House cropped up in the course of the business.

The debate and division were very notable. We all revolted, that is the back-boned Liberals, and we beat the present Government both joined together.

Gladstone and Stafford Northcote both spoke against our doing anything; still we were determined to keep the old Abbey for Englishmen who had done great things for our country, if we could, and I think we have succeeded. So much for the ceremony of giving the Royal Assent to Bills. We are a wonderfully Conservative people.

That such forms should remain all these centuries so punctiliously performed, in these days of activity and bustle, with railways rattling along, telegraphs flashing, etc., is a great marvel. They put one in mind of a fly in amber. With kind love, etc. Chas. H. James.

XXXXXXXXXX

24th. July 1880. Inns of Court Hotel, Holborn, W.C.
My Dear Mary,
Saturday, the members' holiday, has come round again, and having no one to talk to, 'tis pleasant to sit and gossip in writing. I don't think you will get much political instruction from my notes. The newspapers do that much better; but there are certain peculiarities in the House, and in the ways and methods of M.P.'s, which the outside world knows little about. Now, as to my introduction to the House itself, my being sworn in, &c, you may be glad to hear something. Mr. Richard and myself went down towards 'the House' an hour or so before the time for assembling.

When we got there, there were lots before us, everybody shaking hands with everybody else that he had any acquaintance with, all beaming with joy that he had come out of the charge of the six hundred alive, congratulating each other with much effusion, sometimes old friends, who had nearly bitten the dust, being ready almost to embrace each other. New members were, of course, a little awe-stricken, introduced as they were to a heap of new people, it was almost impossible to remember.

There we were, a sort of mob chatting and laughing; no order or anything else, mere chaos; indeed we were nothing till we were sworn and Speaker chosen. I began to wonder how we were to get constituted. Seeing I had been at work like a slave for three weeks to get elected, I thought it was some one's business to see that I was the person so elected. Not a bit of it! I was asked for no credentials, no affidavit of identity. In fact I was with all the others taken on trust. If I had gone to the Court of Chancery to get out £10, I should have had to swear I was the proper man; very likely some one else would have to swear to it too, and a quantity of good ink and paper would have been wasted in such an operation. Here, however, there was nothing of the kind. By and by the Black Rod comes upon the scene, but before him three gentlemen in wigs and gowns had come in and seated themselves at the table immediately before the Speaker's chair. Black Rod in the accustomed language told the Clerk that we were wanted in the House of Lords to hear a message from the Queen, whereupon the Clerk marches off and the mob of members after him. I did not go. If I had then thought of these notes, I think I should have gone; but the crowd was so great there would have been little chance of my seeing or hearing anything. However, they got safe there, and came back, and we were told that her Majesty directed us to elect a Speaker, and to present him to her Majesty next day for approbation. Then for the first time we sit down as it were to business. The Clerk sits at the table. He is not a member, so he has no right to speak. It is therefore necessary that there should be a little dumb

108

show. He is exactly like the Chairman of a meeting who happened to be dumb. So he points with his finger to a member, who gets up and proposes a Speaker. This having been done in a poor grandiloquent sort of speech, he points (ie. our dumb Chairman points) to another member on the other side of the House, and he in a very neat good speech, well delivered, seconded the nomination.

No one proposed another candidate, so he (Mr. Brand, the member for Cambridgeshire, a country gentleman sort of man) was elected. Thereupon his proposer and seconder come and conduct him to his chair. He then seats himself, thanks the House for the honour done him, and sits in the chair, whereupon the mace is put upon the table. Thus we created the first commoner in England in the Parliament of 1880. A couple of members congratulated the Speaker-elect on his advancement. He then declared the House adjourned till the next day. As yet, you will observe, no one has been sworn, and we were in a sort of chrysalis state, neither grub nor butterfly, till the Queen was pleased to confirm the appointment we made. The mace seems solid gold. 'Tis about four feet long; it is a very important article in the constitution of the House of Commons. When *the House* is sitting, as distinguished from its *sitting in Committee*, the mace is on the table. When we are sitting in Committee, and the Speaker is not in the chair, but the Chairman of Committees is in the chair - not *the chair* remember where Mr. Speaker alone sits - the mace is put on a ledge under the table. The Chairman of Committees sits on *a chair* at the table. So I conclude, like a servant-maid's letter, 'so no more at present, hoping you is all well'. I remain, my dear Mary, &c., Chas. H. James.

A servant-maid's letter is nothing without a postscript. I generally manage to sit near the same place. Now that we are toning down, there is no great difficulty about places. You must suppose Mr. Speaker sitting in his chair, then the ministers sit on the front bench on his right hand side. The ex-ministers sit on the left-hand side. Regular ministerial supporters sit behind the ministers. Other general supporters, but who feel free to act otherwise occasionally, sit below the gangway, a line across the benches a third way down the House. The benches don't run continuously there. 'Tis a passage, a gangway.

XXXXXXXXXX

7th. August 1880. Inns of Court, Holborn,W.C.
My Dear Mary,
I presume from Sarah's letter that you are by this time home again. I almost forget where I left off in my account of my parliamentary experience; I think I had got the Speaker appointed, but not sworn; I will assume that I had got so far. Up to this time we were a mob of six hundred gentlemen, with no power, no organisation, no spokesman. We are however beginning to organise ourselves. The next step in this process is swearing the Speaker. The Clerk of the House sees the Speaker take the oath. On this occasion there are tables laid along the floor of the House in the middle, with a number of New Testaments upon them, and the Clerk proceeds to call members for counties, in a certain order, then members for boroughs, &c., and such members go up to the tables, take a book and are sworn. Having been sworn, each goes up to the table of the House with the Clerk of Parliament, and signs his name in a book; he is then marched up to the Speaker, who is sitting in his chair, and he shakes hands with each. The member thereupon walks away behind the Speaker's chair, and comes back into the House through the main entrance, having traversed the lobbies, and takes his seat.

Till forty members are sworn there can be no House; and with reference to difficulties which afterwards arise, with respect to Bradlaugh (2), if he had walked up and taken the oath with the first forty there would, it is conceived, have been no authority to stop him. In the debate about Bradlaugh a good deal was said about the swearing being very much of a farce; it certainly to me seemed to partake of that character. We crowded to the table; we laughed and joked and talked, and it was certainly far removed from anything like seriousness. As yet no member of the Ministry (churchman?) was present; for they, having accepted office under the Crown, had thereby vacated their seats, and had to be re-elected.

A large number of members having been sworn, Black Rod comes and summons the House to the House of Lords to hear Her Gracious Majesty's speech read. I did not happen to be present at this performance, but the House having heard it, and the Speaker having read it from the chair, two members move an address in answer. The mover and seconder of the address do so either in uniform or in full dress. I can't describe exactly what happened on the occasion of the speech, address, &c., because I had not arrived on the scene to take my seat permanently.

In the early part of a new Parliament there is sometimes a good deal of merriment over mistakes made by new members. One of the rules of the House is that no member shall pass between a member while he is speaking and the chair. This rule was little known at first. When any one commits a breach of it, 'tis made known by the other members shouting out 'Order, order, order'. Occasionally it made good fun. One distinguished sort of member was proceeding to his place, and happened to go between the Speaker and the member addressing the House. 'Order, order, order' was shouted (this is done especially by the Tories if the erring member is a Liberal). The poor member did not know what in the world was the matter, or what he had done amiss. So he ran back, thus committing a fresh breach, whereupon 'Order, order, order' went out ten times louder than before, and all the House bursting with laughter. The poor member looked about bewildered and helpless, not knowing what on earth to be at, till at last he sat himself down on the steps in the gangway, till afterwards, when he had courage to get away, some friend explained what it was all about. This is a rule the House is very particular about. No one must pass between the chair and a member speaking.

Another rule that I see observed, and very properly, with great strictness: only one member must be on his legs at the same time to speak. If a member is speaking and another member calls him to order, or rather draws the attention of the Speaker to call him to order, the member originally speaking must sit down. When Mr. Speaker rises, the member in possession of the House, that is, speaking, instantly sits down. One of the most reverential rules of the House is that the House supports the Speaker. All sides of the House do this with great loyalty.

I will end this letter by describing the commencement of business on any ordinary day. The House is supposed to meet at a quarter to four. You go down to the House, if you want to secure a good place during the evening, about half past three; go to a place which is convenient (most members sit nearly about the same place day by day). I have put C.H.J. on the place near where I sit. You leave your hat there, then go to the table where there are cards with the words 'Prayers' inscribed on them. You put your name on one of these cards, and put it in your pocket. Usually the member then goes to a little office, where he gets a paper containing a programme of the business of the day; he thereupon returns to his seat. By and by the old gentleman who sits at the door comes into the House and shouts 'Speaker'. Immediately afterwards the Speaker walks in, accompanied by the Sergeant-at-Arms with the mace on his shoulder, and by the Speaker's chaplain. We all stand up as the Speaker enters, and make our obeisance as he goes by. The Sergeant-at-Arms puts the mace on the table; the Chaplain and Mr. Speaker stand at the table immediately in front of the chair. The Chaplain commences reading the prayers, which are very impressive and appropriate though short. The Speaker makes one response like a clerk in the course of the prayer. We are all standing at first with our faces towards the floor of the House; at a certain point, when the real prayer commences, we all turn. The prayers over, we put our tickets in a little brass holder at the back of our seats, and have so secured them for the evening; the Chaplain retires, walking backwards, and bowing twice. Yours affectionately, Chas. H. James.

XXXXXXXXXX

12th. August 1880. Inns of Court Hotel, Holborn,W.C.
My Dear Mary,
I hope to be down by the 11.45 train on Saturday arriving at Bristol Station at 2.21. I shall come thence by fly. I proceed with a 'Saturday' letter, as I have a spare hour or two this morning. I am wide awake. You need not trouble yourself to write me long letters in answer to these, a post card will be quite enough: I write them to amuse myself, and I don't think I should inflict on you the labour of writing elaborate replies, or indeed replies of any sort, except the very shortest, showing that the lucubration (literary composition) had come to hand.

The City of London has some peculiar privileges about which it is very tenacious. Its Mayor, with that, I believe, of York and one or two other cities of the kingdom, is Lord Mayor. The Queen does not go into the City without asking permission at the City gates, as the House of Lords' Black Rod has to ask permission to enter the House of Commons. It has its own Sheriff and is a County of itself. This privilege, however, it shares with many other cities, your own, Bristol, amongst the number. One of its privileges (which it shares with Dublin) is that it has the right to present its own petitions at the Bar of the House by the hand of the Sheriff.

I was eye-witness to this the other day. At the time of presenting petitions one day I saw some little commotion, and horror of horrors, I saw the Sergeant-at-Arms shoulder the mace, and walk away with it on his shoulder down the House, the speaker sitting in his chair as solidly as a statue. I expected that some terrible event was going to happen, and could not conceive what. When at the door of the House the Sergeant stopped and in

110

walked with him three gentlemen, two of them most wonderfully got up. Scarlet robes of most ample dimensions enveloped them, hats of wondrous shape in their hands. Their robes were trimmed with costly furs, and altogether they made a brave show. These were the Sheriffs of London. The third gentleman was in the ordinary wig and gown of a barrister, the recorder of the City, I presume. Directly that the Sergeant-at-Arms had passed the place where the bar is supposed to be, one of the attendants whips out the bar, which in this case is literally a bar drawn across the entrance, where I expect I have marked it on the plan, or can do again if I have omitted to do so. So now we have these gorgeous gentlemen standing at the bar. The Sergeant-at-Arms on their right hand, with the mace upon his shoulder, the members seated in their places, and Mr. Speaker sitting in his chair. Whereupon Mr. Speaker says 'What have you got there? and one of the Sheriffs, reading from a something in a little frame of some sort, responded, 'Mr. Speaker, Sir, We have a petition from the Lord Mayor, Commomalty, &c., (whatever the Londoners call themselves) of the City of London against trading by the Servants of the State'. This gentleman had the petition in his hand. They made their bows and turned to walk away. The Clerk of Parliament had walked up towards the bar to receive the petition, but unfortunately Mr. Sheriff, having delivered his little speech, had forgotten all about his petition, so some one had to pluck him by his robes to remind him of it, and he turned back on his heel and delivered it to the clerk and vanished. The bar was pushed like a telescope into its place, and the House was in its normal condition. When Mr. Speaker said 'What have you got there?' I thought that we were at the beginning of some child's game, and that there was fun coming - I was however disappointed.

Now about presenting petitions generally, as some of your nieces (that is, after the women have the franchise) or some of your nephews may have to go through the process, I may as well tell you how it is done. Till I came here I had not the slightest notion, or at all events the haziest notion, how it was done. A petition comes up from the country addressed to a member at the House of Commons. It is put in a pigeon-hole by a clerk downstairs under your initial; generally the constituents tell you by letter that it is sent. You get it, read it through to see that there is nothing disrespectful in it, and that it contains the prayer - also to see that it is honestly signed, so far as you can judge by the handwriting. If you find that a number of names are evidently signed by one hand, you should return it. Well, being assured that it is respectful and honestly signed, you put your name to it, so as to show that you presented it. Having come to this point you may treat it in one of two ways.

You may stand up in your place, state who it is from, read the prayer, and the prayer only, and ask leave to present it. This course is very seldom adopted. The other course is at a certain time before half-past five, I think; drop it into a bag hanging by the side of the table, having first given the particulars of the petition in duplicate, in writing to one of the attendants, who hands one to the Committee on Petitions, and the other to a representative of the press, whence it gets into the newspapers. I am not sure whether I have told you that Mr. Speaker wears a silk gown like a Queen's Counsel, and full-bottomed wig of ample dimensions. Ladies always like to   know something about how people are dressed. The Sergeant-at-Arms wears a sword, is dressed in black, wears breeches and black silk stockings, buckles in his shoes, and altogether makes a respectable appearance. I see I am come to the end of my paper, so with kind love, &c., Chas. H. James.

XXXXXXXXXX

21st. August 1880. Inns of Court Hotel, Holborn, W.C.
My Dear Mary,
Here's another of my Saturday letters, but written on a Friday, as I shall tomorrow be, I hope, whisking through the country towards Blaenavon.

I described, I think, in my last how we present petitions. By an association of ideas this reminds me of something that took place forty two or forty three years ago - forty two years ago, what a gulf to look across! Well 'tis about what happened forty two years ago I am in part to speak, and the circumstance puts me in mind that my experience, in a certain way, is perfectly unique amongst members of Parliament. You must know that I was then a law student, a Radical, living in London.

A person of the name of Blewitt was member for Newport in Monmouthshire. He gave notice in the House of Commons that he would move certain resolutions, affirming household suffrage, vote by ballot, and some other remedies of the extreme Radical school; and I determined, if possible, to hear this champion from   our own district enforce his views upon the House. I armed myself with an order for the House of Commons and down I

111

went. At that time politics ran high, so the House was full. In time up got Mr. Blewitt and in a fair speech launched his resolution.

Sir Robert Peel got up and literally laughed them out of the House. I forget whether 'twas in the same debate or not, but on the same evening I heard Lord John Russell (3), Sir Francis Burdett (4) and Daniel O'Connell (5). The last (O'Connell) I heard in this connection. It is a rule of the House of Commons that a petition must only contain statements of fact (not mere reasoning) and a prayer. O'Connell had presented a petition on some matter which at that time excited strong political feeling, and required that it should be read at the table of the House. Sir Robert Peel got up and objected, stating as the ground of his objection that the petition contained reasons. Then the great Daniel arose, and in his fine rich Irish brogue made a telling speech, part of which was 'The honourable baronet objects to receiving this petition because it has reason in it; that, Mr. Speaker, is exactly the reason why I think that it should be received, namely, that it has got reason in it'. The House, however, would not have it.

That, and the fact that on the same evening I heard Sir Robert Peel, Lord John Russell, Sir Francis Burdett and Daniel O'Connell , are all that I remember of that night two and forty years ago. And now for my unique experience. *I never was in the House on any occasion while the House sat from that night till the day I entered at the front door as the member for my native town.* I can't find that any of my friends have had such a curious experience. I have been a strong politician all my lifetime, and I can't explain why I let forty two years of my life pass over me without ever visiting the House during its time of sitting; but there's the fact.

Now we jump over the forty two years and give you what happened on Wednesday, as it explains, after an odd fashion, how we do our work. Alfred came here on Wednesday. The House, according to its wont, on that day was to meet at twelve o'clock. We (Alfy and I) walked down, and being a little early I exercised my privilege in walking him through the library. As we had reached its end, I heard the electric bells ringing away, and I knew at once that members were wanted in the House. On the instant up comes one of the Whips on our side, saying 'pray get into the House at once; we want about ten to make up the House'. He ran about from one to the other, and all the Liberals rushed off, walking through the corridors as fast as we could and into the House to a seat. Within a minute Mr. Speaker was standing on the steps leading to the chair, and with his three-cornered hat (I have forgotten whether I mentioned his three-cornered hat before) he reckoned his men, and finding forty thieves there, he sits in the chair and proceeds with his work. No wonder I never mentioned his hat before; I never saw him wear it or use it, except in counting the House, as it is called. I don't know where he keeps it when he is in the chair, or what it is for except for counting. If we had not mustered forty the day would have been lost to business; as it was we did a fair amount. We had a debate extending over five hours on the Employers' Liability Bill, the third reading of which we passed, and partly went through a Savings Bank Bill, the intent of which is to save old Savings Banks from loss.

Last night we were all night till two in the morning discussing 'Hares and Rabbits'. In my opinion all the hares and rabbits in the country were not worth the time and temper spent and spoiled over them in that one night's debate.

Tonight we resume Hares and Rabbits, and tomorrow the more congenial and less heated atmosphere of Abergavenny and Blaenavon will, I hope, brace me up for the final battles of the campaign. Lord Hartington is now in charge of the House, and he is a very cool customer, as one might say if slang were permissible in a Saturday letter. He seems pretty determined to give the House no hope of rest till it has done substantially the work that is set before it; at this the Tories are very fractious, and the stout Liberals are equally jubilant. With kind love to all, I remain, Yours affectionately, Chas. H. James.

XXXXXXXXXX

29th. August 1880. Inns of Court Hotel, Holborn, W.C.

My Dear Mary,

I indite another Saturday letter, but they are Saturday letters lately by a fiction, for yesterday I was sitting in the House from 12 at noon to 11.30 at night fighting over the Burials Bill, which we carried, and altered so as to make it more palatable to the Nonconformists than the way in which the Lords left it, but possibly to be realtered and spoiled once more by that august body, which we know, in our House, as 'another place'. They have already rejected a Bill to save Irish tenants from great injustice. They have picked the plum out of the Employers'

Liability Bill, and if they insist on their amendments in the Burial Bill, they are preparing a lively time for themselves. We have had some slight experience of obstruction, pure and simple, which kept the House sitting for twenty one hours consecutively; and, as it is to be hoped that in a few years such a thing will be impossible, I may as well explain what obstruction means, and how it is carried out.

One of the great privileges of the House of Commons is that grievances may be complained of before supply is granted. It is the business of the Government to bring before the House all Estimates of the money they require for the coming year, for the various departments. For instance, for the Army and Navy, for the Courts of Justice, for the various public buildings, &c.; and when any vote is asked it is the privilege of any member to bring forward any grievance, which he conceives the people labour under in connection with the institution for which the money is required.

Thus when the vote of money is sought for maintaining say the British Museum, any member may raise a discussion on the management of that institution, and so with regard to any of the institutions of the country. Inasmuch as money must be asked for each year with respect to every institution, this gives members the opportunity of airing any and every grievance they have, so far as the government of the country is concerned, according to the existing law. Parliament is very jealous of the right. 'Tis the weapon which in the reign of Charles the First enabled the great patriots of that day to win our liberties for us, and we are as timid as girls in doing anything which will imperil this right. This is the feeling which makes our Governments so long-suffering in bearing with Irish obstructives.

Well, now to describe what happened on the occasion of our twenty one hours' sitting. The vote before the House was that for maintaining the Irish Constabulary, and the Irish were quite within their right in criticising that vote at length and strictly. Their great objection to the vote was, and is, this. The Irish Constabulary is, they say, the police force for Ireland; but that body is armed as a soldier is armed, he has arms of precision and bayonets, is drilled, as soldiers are drilled, ostentatiously in the eyes of the people. The Irish members, at all events the extreme Home Rule members, about thirty in number, object to this, and claim that they should be disarmed, and the baton take the place of the rifle and bayonet; that their numbers should be diminished, and that they should, in every respect, be put upon the same footing as the English police, and further, that they should not be used in assisting to serve or execute civil process, such as that for recovering rent by distress, or evicting a tenant for non-payment of rent.

The action of the House of Lords about the Irish Disturbance Bill has made the feeling of the Irish members very bitter, and they wish to wreak their vengeance against English governors by preventing, so far as possible, the passing of the particular vote and the forms of the House kept up, as I explained before, because under peculiar circumstances it may yet be a great safeguard of English liberties and give great facilities for carrying out such a project. To succeed in such a course would make government impossible. The Home Ruler aims at that so as to get his own Parliament, while English and Scotch members are equally resolute that they shall not succeed. For some hours the debate went on in what one might say a proper course and order. At length it became apparent that the discussion was not a discussion upon the vote, but was an irritating talk to prevent anything being done.

We were in Committee, the same member may speak as many times as he likes, and Irishmen can talk interminably, so there seemed no reason why the talk might not go on for a fortnight. The tactics of the Irishmen became transparent about one in the morning, and at two measures were devised for keeping the House sitting continuously till the votes were passed, or some reasonable compromise effected. At two o'clock the whip came to me and some others and arranged that we should go to bed and be back at nine in the morning. So away I went, got into bed about half past two, was called at eight, was down in the House again by a quarter past nine. On my way I met two or three members coming from the House, looking very seedy, and when I got down I found them talking away and on precisely the same position, so far as business was concerned, as I had left them some seven hours before. The regular Chairman had gone to rest and a new chairman was appointed. The Irishmen were twelve in number, the remainder having also gone to rest, and we were apparently beginning a struggle of physical endurance. As we were four or five times their number, we must have beaten (them).

At length, however, a truce was come to, the wild Irishmen agreeing to let a number of votes pass on the night of that day, and on Monday they undertook that the Constabulary Vote should pass, and they had another full evening for its discussion. We shall see whether they will perform faithfully that undertaking. And this is the way we do our business in the House of Commons in 1880. To finish the story of those days or rather, of that day. At one o'clock p.m. the sitting ended which had commenced at four o'clock on the previous evening. At two o'clock, that is an hour afterwards, we were sitting again, and, as I was one of the refreshed ones, I sat on till two o'clock the next morning. The wonder is, how we stand it, but the fact is, 'tis not very hard work for us who merely have to sit and listen. For the ministers 'tis terrible, but we can get into the library or lobbies, write our letters, read the papers, &c. The ministers, however, have changes too; 'tis only while some Bill is on of which they have particular charge that they are in strict attendance. During the Irish business, 'twas poor Mr. Forster (6) bore the brunt of the battle. Upon the whole, I think, we have done very well considering the enormous difficulties in our way at the commencement of the Session. With kind love, &c., C. H. James.

XXXXXXXXXX

4th. September 1880. Inns of Court Hotel, Holborn, W.C.
My Dear Mary,
Thanks for yours of the 2nd. I am getting to the end of my work, and this or the next written, I hope from my own hearth, will be the last of the Saturday letters for the Session. I have yet to describe a 'division', a scene in the House of Lords, and some other odds and ends which possibly I may not be able to crowd into this letter. Just now, however, my mind is full of an exciting scene we had in the House last evening, no less than 'naming' a member, a sort of thing which we supposed a myth; but we found out it was a reality, and we acted upon it.

We were in Committee on the Appropriation Bill, which I may explain is the Bill whereby the money is given to Her Majesty for carrying on the Government. On this Bill it is the privilege of members to move that some or one of the items be omitted, the effect of which would be that the officials, covered by that vote, would not get the salaries for the coming year. The Irish members were much exasperated with the House of Lords, and especially with Lord Redesdale, for having rejected certain Irish Bills without discussion. Indeed the whole Liberal party was very angry with them. In order to show this anger, they - the Irish members - moved that the sum appropriated to the payment of the officials of the House of Lords be omitted. This was very well debated, and divisions had. Of course the Irish were beaten by large majorities, and accepted the defeat.

Then a man of the name of Callan, the member for Louth, got up to object to some of the votes about Catholic Chaplains. It was soon seen that he had 'taken too much' as the phrase is. He talked and talked, and we listened, and listened as I believe only members of Parliament can listen. This man is a rabid ultramontane Catholic, and by and bye in his tipsy way he abused our side of the House, calling us ignorant, intolerant, nonconformist infidels, democrats, and every opprobrious term he could use. He was called to order, was required to withdraw the terms. This he declined, but was again allowed to go on, most of us thinking it was better to let him run down. He goes on again and again as bad as before, one member after another rising to call him to order.

At last Bradlaugh (2), who sits close by me, on his using the word 'infidel', again required that the words should be taken down. It was then put to the vote, whether the words should be taken down. This is a technical matter of procedure. The House seemed to think it had better give Callan another trial, and that course was not taken. By the time we had gone on listening to the most insulting epithets, till at last the Chairman of the Committee, Dr. Lyon Playfair, getting out of all patience, explained to Callan that he should 'name' him. On Callan went again, and was soon as offensive as ever, whereupon the Chairman said, Mr. Callan, I call you to order. Calling him 'Mr. Callan' was naming him, for no one is ever allowed to call any member by his name, only by the name of the place he represents, such as the honourable member for Louth &c.

When Callan was thus named, Lord Hartington (7) got up, cited a Standing Order whereby a person so named be suspended further attendance on the House for that sitting, and moved that the Standing Order be put in force against Mr. Callan. It was put to the vote. We all shouted 'Aye'. There was no one cried 'No' although there were half-a-dozen Irish members in the House. Upon that, the Chairman of Committee stated that he must leave the chair to report the matter to the Speaker. Away he went, Callan sitting in his place, groping for his hat under the seat, which he could not find, and we all talking and wondering how it would end.

In a couple of minutes in comes the Speaker in his wig and gown, looking very stern and awful. The mace is put on the table. He stood in his place. Dr. Playfair stood close by, and said that the Committee has passed a certain resolution against Mr. Callan for disregarding the orders of the Chair, and handed to the Speaker the resolution the Committee had passed. Whereupon Mr. Speaker puts the same resolution to the House. We vote upon it as before; the Speaker declares it carried, and that Mr. Callan is suspended from further attendance on the House

114

during the remainder of the sitting, and he says 'Mr. Callan must withdraw'. Callan marches out as straight as he could manage to go; when half way out he turns round, kisses his hand to us, and vanishes, 'and that is the way the thing was done', as Maskelyne and Cook (8) say.

In a minute or two some friendly member is groping under the seat for Callan's hat. 'Tis fished out, and one of the attendants on the House takes it out to him. I hope that may be the last I shall see of the member for Louth this session, as it is doubtful whether I shall trouble the House on Monday. I go down today to spend a day or two with the Lord Justice and Lady James, who have kindly pressed me to do so, and when I come back on Monday, I hope to pack up my traps and get home on Tuesday.

It is pretty clear I can't finish the story of the session in this letter. I enclose what we call a 'whip' which may be a curiosity to keep with these letters. It is yesterday's. Every morning, besides a heap of papers, every supporter of the Government gets such a whip, and we judge by the number of the underscoring the urgency of the whip. Sometimes 'tis underscored with two lines, sometimes with three. This one I see has four, both matters being really important. I think I have seen five. How many there would be if the existence of the Ministry was at stake, I am sure I can't tell. We had yesterday an attempt to make a 'tack' to a money Bill, and a member 'named', both memorable events. I must explain a 'tack' in another letter.
With kind love, &c., Chas. H. James.

XXXXXXXXXX

11th. September 1880. Brynteg. Merthyr Tydfil.
My Dear Mary,
I am about to finish my Saturday letters, for this session at least. You see I am at home, so I doubt whether this letter will smack so much of the House of Commons as former ones; something depends upon atmosphere and surroundings. You know from the newspapers that the House of Lords gave us representatives which we considered great affronts, which we were anxious to pay back so far as we could. For instance, they rejected a Bill that we had taken infinite pains with; the Compensation for Disturbance Bill, one which I, at all events, thought as righteous a measure as was ever presented to a legislature.

Then, again, they declined to look at another Bill - an Irish one - the Registration of Voters' Bill, on the pretext that it was too late in the session. We could not help these bits of petty spite; they were Irish measures, and my Lords doubtless felt they could throw them overboard with impuniity. They however altered the Burials Bill so as to make it very distasteful to the Nonconformists; and then again they picked the plum out of the Employers' Liability Bill, which angered workmen. These Bills came back to us, and we, the Commons, made short work of their alterations, and put them back as we thought they ought to be. Both these measures were to be discussed in the Lords on the same evening.

Some of us hot Radicals determined to go to the House of Lords (which we have the privilege of doing) to see how they ate humble pie. It had oozed out somehow that they intended going through that pleasant process; so away we went. We stood by the bar. The Burials Bill was on. All the bishops were there, twenty or so I should think, in their lawn sleeves and their gowns. The House is resplendent with gilding, and the seats are all scarlet or crimson (men never know the difference between these; I suppose there is a difference). The bishops sat by themselves on the right hand side of the woolsack. The Lord Chancellor sat on the woolsack. The right reverend gentlemen were nibbling at our amendments, and every now and again the Chancellor, who is Speaker of the House of Lords, got up to explain or defend the clauses. I observed that every time he did so he got off the woolsack, stepped on one side and said what he had to say, and then returned to the woolsack and sat down. You will observe here a difference between the Lords and the Commons. Our Speaker never joins in debate; the Lord Chancellor does, and I believe the woolsack is not technically in the House, therefore when he speaks, he gets off it and speaks from the side.

The Lords, as a whole, were a very quiet lot compared with us. There was not half the life and go in the House that we have. One of our party, seeing a couple of old gentlemen dressed more like farmers than anything else, remarked 'Why are not those old fogies made to dress more like lords than farmers? Both the Bills were gone through in half-an-hour or so, all our amendments adopted without exception; and thus it was we saw my Lords eat humble pie in the session of 1880.

115

Some day, of course, some of your nieces will be members of Parliament, and I will explain for their benefit how we manage what we call our divisions. Having debated a matter till we are tired, say as to the second reading of a Bill, Mr. Speaker gets up in his chair and puts what we call the question thus -- 'The question is that the Bill be read a second time; those who are in favour of it say Aye'. Whereupon a lot of members shout out 'Aye'. 'Those who are against it say No'; then a lot shout out 'No'. Whereupon, if a division is challenged, some of the members will say 'The Noes have it'. Then to test it further Mr. Speaker says 'I think the Ayes have it'; whereupon the members insisting on a division, cry out again, 'The Noes have it', upon which the Speaker says 'Strangers withdraw'.

At this stage the Clerk of Parliament turns a sand-glass, which runs two minutes. One of the attendants shouts 'Division!' electric bells are set ringing all over the House, in the library, the reading-room, the refreshment room; everybody hurries into the House, as he must (if he intends to divide) be in the House before the glass runs down. At the same time while the members are running into the House, and while the glass runs, members may, if they choose, go out of the House, as sometimes it is convenient not to divide. It was only on one occasion I evaded a division. We now suppose that the glass has run down. Immediately afterwards the doors are locked, so that no one can go out or get in, and you must vote one way or the other. Now Mr. Speaker gets up again: 'The question is that this Bill be read a second time; those who are in favour say Aye'. Then there is the same shout of Ayes as before; 'Those who are against it say No'; and the Noes shout again; whereupon the Speaker says 'The Ayes to the right and the Noes to the left; tellers for the Ayes, Lord Kensington and Lord Richard Grosvenor' (the Government whips, and I am here supposing the Government goes Aye); 'The Noes to the left; tellers for the Noes, Mr. Stupid and Mr. Slowcoach'. These we suppose are the Tory tellers.

Thereupon we begin to stream out, and now you must look at the map of the House. The Ayes go through the door behind Mr. Speaker's chair, turn to the left, walk through the lobby on the Speaker's right hand, and at the end of it is a sort of desk.

All the members from A to I go by the clerk on one side, and all from I to Z go by the other clerk. These clerks have before them a printed list of all the members, and as you go by say James, Charles or whatever your name is, and he marks your name thus in pencil, 'James, Charles'. This being done, you go on till you come to a door, a glass door locked, and there we wait, speculating whether we are beaten or not, and who has ratted on that particular division, who ran away, &c. By and bye, generally in a couple of minutes, the door opens, and we file through one by one. The two tellers are there numbering us as we go through. We take off our hats as we go past the teller, and he says twenty-two, or whatever the number may be, as you go through, and you walk into the House through the opposite door to that by which you went out; in this case, that I am describing, we walk in through the front entrance. The Noes go through exactly the same process, going out through the front entrance and coming back through the entrance behind the Speaker's chair.

On our return we go to our places; when all are in the tellers come in and go to the clerk at the table and tell him the numbers. The clerk hands the papers with the numbers to the teller who has the largest number. Then all four tellers meet in the centre of the floor of the House and walk up to the table, making two obeisances as they go. When they come to the table the winning teller says 'The Ayes to the right are 103, the Noes to the left 84'. Thereupon the paper is handed to Mr. Speaker. He gets up and says 'The Ayes to the right are 103, the Noes to the left are 84. So the Ayes have it'. Sometimes there is great excitement over these divisions, then we cheer, crying out 'hear, hear' with all our might. Please tell your nieces, that when they are in the House we never clap our hands and they must not. I never heard a clap in the House.

Divisions are amusing sometimes. Perhaps the dining-rooms may be half full of members dining. Away goes the little bell, up starts the member, leaves his chair against the table, claps on his hat, and away he goes; the waiters rush with the plates to keep them warm, and off we walk. We crowd into the House, ask eagerly what's it all about, are we Ayes or Noes? Sometimes the Whip is near the door, simply saying 'Noes, Noes' or 'Ayes, Ayes', as the case may be. Please observe every question is resolved into Ayes or Noes; we never vote in any other way, and sometimes it is exceedingly difficult to tell whether you are Aye or No. So it is not at all uncommon to find us asking each other are we Ayes or Noes; and thus we make our laws in the British Parliament in the year of grace 1880. Now I think you will be able to instruct your young friends how to get through parliamentary forms as well as most people could.
With kind love, &c., Chas.H. James.

12th. February 1881. Inns of Court Hotel, Holborn, W.C.

My Dear Mary,

I am going to inflict upon you one more Saturday letter at all events. It will be, in part only, about a little revolution that we have been making in Parliament, greater than has been made since Pride's Purge (9) in Cromwell's time. To begin at the beginning: we were fighting the wild Irish about the Coercion Bill. We began the fight at four o'clock on Monday afternoon. I came up from Merthyr that evening, and got to the House about six o'clock, and sat persistently, listening to the most dreary speeches, till seven o'clock next morning. Tuesday morning at seven I was sent home for sleep, charged to come back as soon as I could. About one in the day I was back again. The speeches still going on, adjournments of the debate, adjournments of the House moved, and moved again, with occasional speeches on the main question. On each new motion of adjournment each of the thirty three Irish malcontents had a right to speak afresh. Well, I stayed in the House on Tuesday night till past twelve; then I was told off to be back at nine on Wednesday. I was walking across Palace yard on my return when the clock was striking the hour. As I was going up the staircase to the House I met Healy (a member), secretary to Parnell, running down as fast as feet could carry him. I thought something was happening, so I ran up, and as I went into the House the Speaker was standing before the chair reading from a paper something to this effect, that a small minority had wilfully obstructed the business of the House, and he felt it his duty to the House to decline calling on any more members to speak to the question, but would proceed to a division. The Irish members, about a dozen, put their heads together; they were as pale as ashes, many of them. They all got up in their places shouting 'privilege, privilege, tyranny' &c., then walked out of the House. Thereupon the Speaker put the question, which was carried without a division, and thus we English effected our revolution of the year 1881. It's a vast improvement upon the French way of doing the same thing.

It was further carried out on the next day, but I was in Merthyr (Tydfil) talking to the Odd-Fellows. Now the Speaker has issued his new resolution and matters are going on in a reasonable manner, and I think we have, after wonderful patience, learnt how to stamp out obstruction. The House for awhile is shorn of its ancient glory, but on the whole I think we have established its efficiency once more. So much for that.

One day I observed a little paper stuck about the lobbies about as big as my hand, that Mr. Speaker would hold levees on the 2nd. and 9th. February at ten o'clock p.m., full dress. To one not given to levees or full dress this was a portentous notification. On enquiring I found that every one was expected to go or make some excuse, and that you must appear in a Court suit. So I betook me to Mrs. Richards, who is great in these matters, and she soon put me in the way. I put myself in the hands of a tailor, and he rigged me out as follows: plum-coloured coat and trousers with a certain amount of gilt braiding, with gilt buttons having a crown on them, a white waistcoat with like buttons but smaller, a hat like an admiral's with braid and buttons. This you wear under your arm as a rule. This is one of the regulation suits for the occasion.

Being dressed up thus (ordinary dress shirt and white tie) off I drove in a cab. Of course when we got near we had to fall in line with a lot of carriages and cabs, and the only pleasure of this part of the business was the cabmen chaffing each other. Being set down you walk to a room to leave your great coat or other outside covering. Then you give your name to a stylish sort of gentleman, who ticks you off on the printed paper that they use on division lists!! I thought it smelt of the shop a little. I was then handed over to a person to be introduced to Mr. Speaker, when lo and behold this good gentleman was no other than the door-keeper inside the door of the House. Poor fellow, I have seen him on his little stool half dead with sleep many and many a time.

However, on we went, and I was introduced to Mr. Speaker, who shakes you cordially by the hand, and then you mix with the general company, and get hold of any you know to chat to. Two thirds of the people were in red, that is military costume. Mr. Morley was flaming in red, so were the two Lawrences. Some were plum coloured gentry like myself, and we did not look quite as foolish as one might have expected. Then a certain number were in black velvet with bright steel buttons. I thought theirs was the prettiest dress; I am sorry now I did not go in for velvet. However, the thing is done and there's an end of it. My dress, barring accidents, lasts my time.

On two sides of the room were tables with coffee, tea, wine, claret and champagne cup &c., which those who choose took standing. After staying twenty minutes or so you depart; and so ended my first levee. I shan't care or be much worried about future ones. The rooms were handsome, in the general style of the Houses of Parliament; the Speaker's house forms part of the Palace of Westminster. The large panels are filled with portraits of former

Speakers and altogether the rooms seemed to me handsome without being gaudy. To an M.P. Mr. Speaker is the greatest man in existence, as the head master is the greatest man in the world to a public school boy, and I am glad I have paid him the customary respect that is expected of loyal members. Suppose our fathers and mothers and grandfathers could see us sometimes on these occasions, how they would rub their eyes. I find the Lawrences very cordial and kind to me on occasions like this. With kind love and remembrances to all, &c., Chas. H. James.

I don't know whether Sarah will know me in my new toggery.

XXXXXXXXXX

28th. July 1881. Inns of Court Hotel, Holborn, W.C.

My Dear Mary,

My Saturday letters of the last session pretty well exhausted those matters which strike a new member, and therefore presumably those which would interest outsiders. I observe one or two little things which I think had escaped me when I wrote, and which I may as well note down, as a sort of appendix to my former epistles.

First of all, about getting ladies into the Ladies' Gallery. This is a very troublesome operation, as you will see. That gallery holds very few. I don't know the number, but scarcely one tenth of the number seeking to get in, so we have to ballot, which is done after this fashion.

Immediately after prayers, members wishing to ballot rush to the lobby, put their names down on little oblong pieces of paper, fold them up, and hand them to an official, who is surrounded by a struggling mass of members. This is done nominally by handing your paper over the heads of men half a dozen deep, and 'tis handed from one to another till the official gets it. He is at a table with a glass bowl, an ordinary large fish-bowl apparently, before him, into which the papers go. When all the papers are in, he puts in his hand and at haphazard draws out a paper, calls out the name, and another official enters it into a book. All those around see his hand in the bowl, so there can be no hocus-pocus process about it in favour of any one particular man. Having drawn out the full number, there's an end of the business. I was standing by a member one day, who, when the drawing was over, exclaimed with a groan, 'This is the fifteenth time I have tried, and without success'. Suppose you succeeded, and I succeeded once for the Lord Justice's daughter, you have the privilege of admitting two ladies on the week-day following the day of ballot. As very few know for a week in advance what will be on, this prevents an inordinate rush for any particular day, so folks take their chance what sort of an evening's entertainment they get; so that's the way the ladies get in.

Many of the public, I presume, think that members are always sitting in their places listening to arguments and voting as reason impels them when the time comes. Usually, unless Gladstone or Bright or some really good speaker is up, not a third of the members in the House are in that part of the House where the debating goes on. Some are in the reading room reading the papers. Some in the library, or the lobbies, writing letters or reading. Some in the tea room, others again in the dining room eating their dinner.

If a division is called, little electric bells ring all over the House, whereupon every member who intends to divide puts down whatever he is about, walks as fast as he can towards the House. Our time for this is measured by a sandglass, which runs a couple of minutes or so, placed before the clerk at the table. If he has heard nothing of the debate, and perhaps knows nothing of what the division is about, as he goes into the House he passes by the Whip of his party, who says 'Ayes' or 'Noes' as we may happen to be, and so we vote.

The other day I found after I had so voted that I had voted decidedly and unmistakeably against what I should have done, had I known the exact state of things. The next division was virtually the same question in another form, and I voted against the Government. The Whips would be puzzled to know on what principle I went. When all the work of the day is done the Speaker says 'This House doth now adjourn', whereupon the door keeper outside the House shouts out at the top of his voice 'Who goes home?' The members crowd out, rush down the steps, of which we have three or four flights; most go into a sort of cloister where we put up our coats, umbrellas, &c., and march away.

Outside the place men are shouting 'hansom', 'four-wheeler', into which members get. The walking members run across Palace Yard, taking care they don't get run over; the lights on the tower are out, and so the historic House of Commons is dispersed for that day. In summer, when it is daylight, as it often is when we walk home, I

118

hear more larks and thrushes and blackbirds sing from cages hung out here and there, in one morning, than I should hear in Merthyr (Tydfil) for a whole year round.

[In 2004 wild birds, including thrushes and blackbirds, flourish and sing their little hearts out, in Merthyr Tydfil. Members of Merthyr Tydfil & District Naturalists' Society make early starts to hear the inimitable DAWN CHORUS. Ed.]

So much for our ways and doings. When at dinner &c., the bell rings for a division, the scene is comical. The moment the bells begin down go the knives and forks, everybody tips up his chair against the table, the waiters hurry to put the plates away to keep warm, the whole place is deserted. When 'tis over back we come and proceed where we left off, and finish in peace, unless another division should rouse us. As to our present work, Mr. Gladstone has a notion we may get through 'Report' in time to have the third reading of the Land Bill today; I hope he may, but I much fear it.

I hope you and Mary Warren have enjoyed your trip to Tenby, and I trust you will find Christopher improved by the time of your return to Bristol.
With kind love, &c., Chas. H. James.

XXXXXXXXXX

NOTES

(1).   Charles Herbert James, 1817-1890. See *Merthyr Express*. 3.11.1900.p.3; 1.12.1900.p.7; and 15.12.1900.p.3. Also Charles Russell James' Childhood. *Merthyr Historian*. Volume Thirteen. p.123-152.

(2).   Charles Bradlaugh, 1833-1891. Freethinker and radical politician. In 1880 elected Liberal M.P. for Northampton, he was not allowed to sit till 1886 because as an atheist he unsuccessfully claimed the right to affirm instead of taking a meaningless oath. His pen name was Iconoclast. He was an advocate of contraception and was prosecuted for his views.

(3).   Lord John Russell, 1792-1878. English statesman, elected M.P. for Tavistock in 1813.

(4).   Sir Francis Burdett, 1770-1844. Became an M.P. in 1796, witnessed the French Revolution.

(5).   Daniel O'Connell, 1775-1847. An Irish politician, called 'the Liberator'. He was elected M.P. for Co. Clare in 1828. As a Roman Catholic he was ineligible to sit in Parliament, the Government enacted Catholic emancipation.

(6).   William Edward Forster, 1819-1886. English Liberal statesman, Quaker parentage. Became Liberal M.P. for Bradford in 1861. Rose to cabinet rank and in 1870 carried the Elementary Education Act. Under Gladstone, Forster was chief secretary for Ireland, which made him unpopular with Irish members in Parliament. He had Parnell and other Irish leaders arrested, but in the absence of cabinet support they were released in 1882 and Forster resigned. He was strongly opposed to Home Rule in Ireland.

(7).   Lord Hartington, Spencer Compton Cavendish, 1833-1908. 8th. Duke of Cavendish.

(8).   John Nevil Maskelyne, 1839-1917. English magician who was born in Wiltshire, he was in a professional partnership with George Cooke for many years. Maskelyne devoted energy to exposing spiritualistic frauds.

(9).   Thomas Pride, died 1658. A parliamentary colonel in the English Civil War, he was appointed to expel Presbyterian royalist members from Parliament. By 'Pride's Purge' more than one hundred members were expelled.The remaining M.P.s brought Charles I to trial.

XXXXXXXXXX

Photo courtesy of Ceri Thompson, Curator, Coal Mining Collections, National Mining Museum of Wales Blaenavon.

THE MERTHYR RIOTS OF 1816 AND 1831
INTERESTING REMINISCENCES
by
SOLOMON MARKS, CANTON

"In 1816 the Cardiff Cavalry was the only troop in the county of Glamorgan, and consisted of most of the respectable tradesmen and yeomen of the neighbourhood of Cardiff, and was under the command of Major or Colonel John Woods, senior, Captain John Woods, junior, Cardiff; and Lieutenant Samuels, of Bonvilstone. Doctor of the troop was Dr. Hopkins of Llandaff.

THE CALL TO MERTHYR, 1816

"When the troop was called to go to Merthyr, they mustered together in a very short time, and I can say without fear of contradiction by anyone who had a knowledge of them, that they were so well disciplined and perfect in their drill and military movements that they were fit for actual service. Their captain, Mr. John Woods, jun., being a first-class and good officer, and a very strict disciplinarian, he would make the members of the troop attend their drill regularly. The following are, to the best of my recollection, their names: - - Quartermasters Hopkins, of Roose; his two sons; two Lowries, of Cogan Pill; two Holbins; two Hernes, of Whitchurch; French, of Wenvoe; Ballard, of Cowbridge; Rowlands, of Whitchurch; Greatrex, of Michaelston-le-pit; Jenkins, of St. Bride's; Bradley, of Cowbridge; two Phillips's, near Peterston; Loughers, of Cadoxton; Evans, of Fairwater; Evan David, of Radyr; Lewis, of Caerau; Stevens, of Llandaff; Morgan, of Pengam; John, of Plasturton; Sergeant William Bradley, of Cardiff; Joseph Davies, of Cardiff; Edward Davies, of Cardiff; Thomas Watkins, of Cardiff; Landers, Dimond, Sweet, William Vachell, William Bassett, Thomas Hussey, Griffith Lloyd, William Stibbs, senior, Thomas Minnett, J. Bird, printer, Michael Marks, Thomas David, farrier, Lewis, shoemaker, all of Cardiff; Phillips, of Leckwith, trumpeter, and a farmer named Matthews.

"When the troop was leaving Cardiff for Merthyr, the wives of the married men were crying, kissing, and begging of their husbands not to go, fearing they should not see them alive again, feeling sure they would be killed by the rioters; the husbands had very great difficulty to leave Cardiff.

"The staff of the Glamorganshire Militia that went up to Merthyr at the same time, under Captain Ray, were Sergeant-Major Rees, Sergeants Lewis, Lewis, Greenhood, Vaughan, Evans, Evans, Rees, Meyrick, Hughes, Lloyd, Christopher, Hockstoff and Jenkins.

"The members of the band also went and took their guns with them. T. Quelch, Wolsey, Pugh, Hicks, Collings, Prouse, Gregory, Evans, Williams, D. Rees, T. Rees, and Martin Rebusky. These and the Cardiff troop of Cavalry arrived in Merthyr a short time before the regulars came from Brecon, and were set upon by the mob, and would have been badly treated had not the regulars come up. TWO OF THE CAVALRY MEN WERE HURT by some of the rioters throwing large staffs at them. The cavalry brought two chaises full of these staffs they had taken from the mob, to Cardiff, and two of the cavalry men had a pension from the Government, for the injuries they received.

"When the news reached Cardiff that the troop was coming home, the married ladies went to meet their husbands on the North-road, and when they saw them there was a rush and outburst of joy; such kissing and hugging I shall never forget. "After the above riots of 1816 the troop continued under the command of the Woods until 1817 or 1818, when a dispute arose about the cavalry contingent money. A member of the troop wrote to the Government, stating that the troop could not get their contingent money due. In consequence of this the troop was called up, and they mustered and went to Canton Common for parade. Colonel or Major Woods, senior, in command, was riding an Arabian horse, given him by a friend, and by some means Mr. Woods got thrown off and fell upon his sword, and died in a short time after, in consequence of the said accident, but it was proved the contingent money had been paid to all the members of the troop, and the Woods gave up the troop after this.

CARDIFF CAVALRY REFORMED, SEVERAL TIMES

"In the year 1822 or 1824 a gentleman by the name of Whitlock Nicholls, residing at Adamstown, who had been a captain in one of the local volunteer regiments of Glamorganshire, reformed the Cardiff Cavalry after the Woods gave it up. Some of the members of the old troop joined the new in Captain Nicholls's troop; their names were Quartermaster Hopkins and his two sons, William Bradley, Roberts of Roose, and Edward Davis. The new members were Edward Bird, junior, William Bird, junior, George Bird, Bird, John Lloyd, Henry Lloyd, Henry Partridge, James Ewins, John James, William Evans, of Llandaff; Richards, of Llandaff; Daniel Phillips, of Llandaff; Daniel Lloyd, William Lewis, Red Lion; Thomas Yorath, Geek, John Llewellyn, Nathan French, William Morgan, Thomas Daniel Rees, James Yorath, Robertharn, Solomon Marks (author of this note) and others. Several of the above left Captain Nicholls' troop one after the other, and in 1926 he could not muster sufficient men for the Inspector-General to review. In consequence Captain Nicholls gave up the command, and there was no cavalry in Cardiff from then until the year 1828 or 1829, when a new troop was formed under Major Richards, of Llantrissant, and two Moggridges, of Gabalva. This troop was called the Cardiff, Llandaff and Llantrissant Troop, and were combined as one, under the command of Major Richards, of Llantrissant, and Government Troop-Sergeant-Major Castle.

"As Mr. William Morgan (wine merchant, late of Bridgend) and myself (Mr. Solomon Marks, Canton) got together a sufficient number of members to form the Cardiff troop, under the command of Captain John Moggridge, of Gabalva, Mr. William Morgan was appointed quartermaster and I second sergeant. I therefore got myself properly drilled and instructed in the sword exercise, and soon became efficient; so much so, that I undertook to drill recruits, and I at all times (in the absence of John Myers, cornet) acted as cornet to the troop. After it was formed I used to drill the recruits every evening of the week in the Castle Grounds and after the troop was called up and placed under the command of Captain John Moggridge in the early part of 1830.

122

THE 1831 MERTHYR RIOTS

"In 1831, when the Merthyr riots took place, I was not a member of the troop, having left it three months previously. Lord Bute, the then Lord Lieutenant of the county, who was at Cardiff Castle, spoke to a Mr. Robert Thomas, who happened to be with his lordship, and asked Mr. Thomas 'Do you know where I shall find a person to muster the troop of Cardiff Yeomanry Cavalry?' He said 'Yes, my Lord, if he has not gone to Merthyr'. Mr. Thomas mentioned my name to his lordship, who at once sent for me, and asked me if I would take the trouble to get them together, and how I would go. I replied, 'It is no trouble, my lord, but my duty to do so, I have my own stable dress and sword, and if your lordship will give me your warrant and a good horse, I will start at once'.

"I mustered about twenty of the troop and brought them on to the Castle grounds that same evening, and they went up to Newbridge (Pontypridd) to join the other members of the troop that had left Cardiff in the morning, and those from Llantrissant. The Cardiff, Llandaff and Llantrissant troops all met at Newbridge.

"The ammunition was brought from Llantrissant, and they proceeded to Merthyr. The names of the Cardiff troop were Quartermaster W. Morgan, Sergeants Partridge, Ewins and Jones, Corporals Mark Marks and John Thackwell, Privates William Stibbs, jun., Taylor, Matthews, T. Yorath, T. John, Dl. Phillips, Stevan Staurenghi, T. Lodwick, Wm. Williams, John Winstone, Evans, Jenkins, Wheeler, Richards, Spear, T. Morgan, Lewis, Spencer, J. Yorath, Robertharn, Wright, Edward David, farrier; James Richards, trumpeter; and other country members whose names I now forget.

"The Glamorganshire Militia staff that went up to Merthyr, under the command of Captain Howells, were Sergeant-Major Rees, Sergeants Hopkins, Lewis, Lloyd, Evans, Jenkins, Greenhood, Rees, Meyrick.

"The Swansea Cavalry, under the command of Captain Penrice, gave up their swords. Captain Penrice had been in the Battle of Waterloo, and it was he who first gave up his sword to the rioters, and most of the Swansea troop followed his example. In consequence of the Swansea troop giving up their swords to the rioters, the Government disbanded the whole of the Glamorganshire Yeomanry Cavalry, and none were again formed until Mr. C.H. Williams, of Roath Court, formed the 1st. Glamorgan Light Horse Cavalry Volunteers.

"The rioting at Merthyr was very serious, and resulted in one man, by name Dick Penderyn, getting hung at Cardiff, for stabbing one of the 93rd. Highlanders. A man by the name of Abbott, a barber, who resided at Merthyr, and who had served his apprenticeship to a Mr. Hicks (a barber whose shop was in Angel-street, Cardiff, directly opposite the Angel Hotel, and formerly occupied by Mr. William Stibbs, senior). The barber was the principal witness against Dick Penderyn, Abbott swearing he saw Dick stab the Highlander.

"I have, to the best of my recollection, given the names of the Cardiff men who took a prominent part in quelling the riots of 1816 and 1831, and as I before stated, it will doubtless be interesting to learn their names".

(*Merthyr Telegraph.* 18.10.1878.p.3.col.5.)

NEW HARDBACK: LIMITED EDITION

Henry Williams, Lancarvan
By E.W.Cloutman and W.Linnard

This is a detailed study of the life and work of Henry Williams (1727–1790), a farmer/clockmaker who produced some of the finest domestic clocks ever made in Wales. Apprenticed in Gloucester, but subsequently working in the little village of Llancarfan in the Vale of Glamorgan, Henry Williams was a remarkable and versatile clockmaker.

This lavishly illustrated book describes in detail all his known clocks, and presents a penetrating analysis of their stylistic features. The clocks include a month-going longcase clock, ten eight-day longcase clocks (three of them with tidal dials), two thirty-hour longcase clocks (one with alarm), and a fine bracket clock as well as silver watches.

The study reveals a connection between Henry Williams and the Bilbie family of clockmakers in Somerset, which gives important new insights into clock-dial manufacture and dial engraving in the eighteenth century. It also shows the relationships and social status of this master craftsman within the rural community in the 'Garden of Wales'.

This book is a major contribution to the study of clockmaking in the eighteenth century and provides a unique picture of contemporary life in the Vale of Glamorgan.

This first edition is strictly limited to 300 individually numbered copies. It consists of 136 pages, hardback, with 180 illustrations and 4 colour plates. Price £21.00. For ordering details see overleaf.

Published by Tathan Books, PO Box 6044, Radyr, Cardiff CF15 8YS.